Almaguin Chronicles
Memories of the Past

Almaguin Chronicles
Memories of the Past

Astrid Taim

NATURAL HERITAGE BOOKS
A MEMBER OF THE DUNDURN GROUP
TORONTO

Copyright © 2008 Astrid Taim

All rights reserved. No part of this publication may be reproduced, stored in a retrieval system, or transmitted in any form or by any means, electronic, mechanic, photocopying or otherwise (except for brief passages for purposes of review) without the prior permission of Dundurn Press. Permission to photocopy should be requested from Access Copyright.

Published by Natural Heritage Books
A Member of The Dundurn Group
3 Church Street, Suite 500
Toronto, Ontario, M5E 1M2, Canada
www.dundurn.com

Library and Archives Canada Cataloguing in Publication

Taim, Astrid
    Almaguin chronicles : memories of the past / Astrid Taim.

Includes index.
ISBN 978-1-55002-760-0

    1. Almaguin Highlands (Ont.)--History. 2. Frontier and pioneer life--Ontario--Parry Sound (District). 3. Logging--Ontario--Parry Sound (District)--History. I. Title.

FC3095.A453T342 2007   971.3'15   C2007-904653-3

1   2   3   4   5   11   10   09   08   07

Front cover: top, Johnstone's Tourist Camp, courtesy of Burk's Falls and District Museum; bottom (l) Paddling near Lost Channel, courtesy of Glenn Kirton; The Kawigamog on the Pickerel River, courtestsy of Burk's Falls and District Museum. Back cover: Sport fishing in the Loring area, courtesy of Glenn Kirton.
Cover and text design by Erin Mallory
Edited by Jane Gibson

Care has been taken to trace the ownership of copyright material used in this book. The author and the publisher welcome any information enabling them to rectify any references or credits in subsequent editions.
J. Kirk Howard, President

We acknowledge the support of the **Canada Council for the Arts** and the **Ontario Arts Council** for our publishing program. We also acknowledge the financial support of the **Government of Canada** through the **Book Publishing Industry Development Program** and **The Association for the Export of Canadian Books** and the **Government of Canada** through the **Ontario Book Publishers Tax Credit Program** and the **Ontario Media Development Corporation**.

In memory of my mother Sally who was my best friend. I will miss her terribly.
November 27, 2006.

What is dedication?
To give up a part of one's life
To achieve an ultimate goal.

— Camp Chikopi, Ahmic Harbour, Ontario, June, 2005.

Table of Contents

Acknowledgements 8
Foreword — Away Up North 9
Introduction 11

One — A Settler's Story: The Founding of Burk's Falls 21
Two — Pioneer Adventures: The Arrival of the Train 32
Three — The Life of a River Driver 40
Four — A Century of Child Care in the Parry Sound District 52
Five — The South River Connection 60
Six — Arthur G. Peuchen: A Survivor 74
Seven — Pickerel River Logging Days 77
Eight — Lost Channel: A Company Town 87
Nine — The Last Stands 98
Ten — The Walton Family: Boat Builders 102
Eleven — A Life Remembered: Richard Thomas (1932–2006) 113
Twelve — A Boy Scout's Journey and Lake Cecebe's Green Bay 121
Thirteen — Kearney: Home of Ontario Baseball Champions 134
Fourteen — Sundridge and the Johnstone Story 139
Fifteen — Galna Bridge: The Bridge That Will Stand Forever 147

Epilogue 150
Appendix A — Poems and Songs of Clarence Brazier 152
Appendix B —"Trouble on the Tote Road" by Everett Kirton 159
Appendix C — Selected Writings by Richard Thomas 161
Notes 164
Bibliography 174
Index 176
About the Author 191

Acknowledgements

I would like to thank the following individuals/organizations for their assistance and support in what seemed to be my never-ending research of this second book project: the Burk's Falls and District Historical Society and its president Betty Caldwell, the Nipissing Township Museum and its curator Joe Steele, the Perry Township Public Library and head librarian Pat Aitchison, the South River-Machar Union Public Library, the Sundridge-Strong Union Public Library, Gail (Stringer) Maeck of South River, Art Loney of South River, Elwood Addison of Burk's Falls, the late Sylvia Maw of Burk's Falls, Jane Anderson of Sundridge, the Johnstone family of Sundridge, Clarence Brazier of Sprucedale, Barry Cott of Station Studios, Doug Mackey of Chisholm Township, former mayor of the Town of Kearney, Cliff Reeds and his wife, the late Claudia Reeds, Jenny Thomas of Armour Township, Glenn Kirton of Bracebridge and Bill Walton of North Bay. Special thanks go to Peter Barr, former publisher of the *Almaguin News* (*Almaguin Publishing* (1989) Limited) in Burk's Falls, for allowing me access to the newspaper's archives and to Mary Johnston, formerly of the *Almaguin News* (*Almaguin Publishing* (1989) Limited), for hauling those archives up and down the stairs for me!

As well much appreciation goes to Stephen Heder, "retired" supervisor for the Nipissing-Parry Sound Child Adoption, Foster Care and Child Abuse Prevention branch for providing the historical information on the early years of the Children's Aid Society in Burk's Falls.

For their generosity in allowing me the use of photographs/artwork in their possession, I thank the following: the Burk's Falls and District Museum, Elwood Addison of Burk's Falls, Jane Anderson of Sundridge, Betty Caldwell of Burk's Falls, Mendelson Joe of Perry Township, the Johnstone family of Sundridge, Gail (Stringer) Maeck of South River, Glenn Kirton of Bracebridge and the late Claudia Reeds of Kearney.

And finally to my mother Sally for her continued patience with me right up until her death in November 2006, and to my book publisher Barry Penhale for never giving up on me!

Foreword: Away Up North

The fair Far North holds a charm for me,
Away up North's where I long to be.
Where the quiet lakes, through the dreaming night,
Mirror the shores in silvery light,
When a sentinel moon sails a cloudless sky,
And the bull frogs croak, and the night-birds,
                          Away up North.

Away up North where the heights are steep,
Where the trails are long and the canyons deep,
Where the frosts are keen and the snows are white,
Where the huskies howl to the pulsing night,
Where work is work and rest is sweet,
Where strong men strive and defy defeat,
                          Away up North.

Away up North where the spruce and pines
Keep a steadfast guard, where the woodchuck mines,
Where the birches sway and the hills around
Are laughing back each wildwood sound,
Where the mountains tower and campfires glow,
Where the waters swirl and the mad winds blow,
                          Away up North.

Away up North there's a little shack
By a tamarack swamp, and it called me back;
There's a friendly pine by my cabin door,

And I seems to hear it o'er and o'er,
Whisper, and croon, and sigh to me,
>   Away up North.

Oh, the Lone Land calls, and I know she waits;
I forsake the lusts, the greeds, and hates,
For tonight, me thinks, my kit I'll pack,
And at early dawn I'll be hiking back
To the fair far North, where my soul finds rest,
>   Away up North.[1]

Introduction

Although the Grand Trunk Railroad had extended its line from Gravenhurst to North Bay in the late 1880s, by 1900 the northern most areas of the District of Parry Sound were still not accessible by even a conventional roadway. Homesteaders, their claims precariously strung along the Pickerel River, relied on the waterway as their transportation route—much like the settlers south of them had depended on the Magnetawan River years before. For those living in the northern wilderness, the closest centre with a railway was the Town of Parry Sound. Here, larger quantities of supplies could be purchased and then transported by the occasional steamboat that navigated the narrow channels and lakes along the Pickerel River. But, as the steamboats became an integral part of the area's booming logging industry, additional vessels were built. They were now needed to transport more than just lumberjacks and supplies. The Pickerel River was rapidly becoming an attraction for sportsmen.[1]

What we know of the heyday of this waterway comes from the writings of the people who had firsthand experience with the river. For instance, after the First World War, the deer-hunting season in the fall was often the busiest. Around 1916–17 the most famous of the northern steamers, the *Kawigamog*, averaged about forty hunters over a season. But by 1921, the year in which a hunter could bag two deer with one licence, over 1,000 hunters boarded the steamer—and reportedly returned with approximately the same number of deer!

With both the Muskoka area and the southern Parry Sound District having been inundated by sportsmen from southern Ontario and the United States by the turn of the 20th century, the next logical step for the more adventuresome sportsman was to venture even further north. To reach Lost Channel and the Key Valley, the hunters would travel by Canadian National Railway's "colonist" cars, basically just freight cars or rented coaches. These hunters, coming from such diverse hometowns as St. Thomas, Hamilton, Brantford, Buffalo and Toronto, would pack their assorted gear on these particular train cars. The cars would arrive at Lost Channel to be unloaded and then parked at the siding just south of the mill until the men were ready to return home. There is one story where twenty-two colonist cars loaded with hunters pulled into Lost Channel, in addition to the hunting parties already on board the regular passenger train. As well, the *Kawigamog* was packed to capacity, with a large barge tied alongside. The hunters aboard the steamboat were put on shore wherever they wanted, while other still were taken directly to established hunt camps. A journey like this would last well after midnight. Once at Port Loring, just east of Lost Channel, the remaining hunters would disembark with the *Kawigamog* continuing on to Duck Lake.[2]

We are truly grateful to the individuals who had the foresight to ensure that their memories of these early years were recorded for posterity—in particular, memories of those pioneers-turned-writers Everett Kirton (b. 1894 – d. 1984), and Aubrey "Dob" Walton (b. 1907 – d. 1997).

Everett Kirton, pioneer-turned-writer, married Elma Ward of St. Thomas in October 1927. The couple moved from Loring to Powassan in 1949 where Everett became a division clerk for the Department of Lands and Forests. Upon his retirement in March of 1964, he began writing his memoirs.

Their recollections of life along the Pickerel River at the turn of the 20th century remain the most accurate record available of the area, particularly of Lost Channel, to survive to the present day. Then there are the authentic memories of people like Clarence Brazier, who was born in the Magnetawan area in the early the 20th century. Clarence became a river driver at a very young age, even working for a time on the Pickerel River for the Schroeder Mills and Timber Company. But it was Everett Kirton who first began writing down what he remembered of the settling of northern Parry Sound District. Retired by the 1960s and living his final years in Powassan, he maintained that society owed a great debt to the pioneers who made their homes in this wilderness. His manuscripts, although never published, were intended to perpetuate their memory and be a tribute to their contributions.[3]

In 1978, Dob Walton, a member of the well-known family of late 19th century boatbuilders, granted an interview with the *Almaguin News*. The resulting article gave readers a whole new outlook on the importance of the steamboats in those early years. At the time of the interview he was living in Powassan with his wife Mildred, and they were about to celebrate their 60th wedding anniversary. As readers would discover, Dob had the great fortune to grow up in the steamboat era, working on the Pickerel River for a total of twenty years. Once he was old enough, he went to work on a boat under the watchful eye of his grandfather, Captain Arthur Walton. The young Dob was once quoted as stating that his grandfather was his hero. "I hope I can reflect some of his life in mine." Although the subsequent newspaper articles were mainly on the Walton steamer, the *Kawigamog* (the Native word for "where the waters turn back"), Dob still manages to paint an extraordinary picture of what life was like for the people living along this river. The story of *Kawigamog* first appeared in *Almaguin News* during the summer of 1978, and was reprinted in its entirety in 1996 to be read by a whole new audience. Although the *Kawigamog* travelled along the seventy-kilometre route between Port-of-Loring (also called Port Loring) and the railhead at Lost Channel during the years between 1913 and 1928, in actuality, the Walton family first began building boats back in the 1880s in the southern portion of the District of Parry Sound.

Arthur Walton started his boat business in 1886. His first steamer was the *Lady Katrine*, built in the southern Almaguin Highlands community of Katrine. But it wasn't until the 1890s during the golden age of shipbuilding in Almaguin that the Walton family became the most prominent of the steamboat owners operating on the Magnetawan River. In 1890 and the following year, the *Emulator* and the *Glen Rosa* were built by Arthur Walton and his sons William and Edgar, along with family friend Sam Best. But, less than twenty years later in 1908, both steamers, no longer competitive with the newer steamers being built, would be demolished for scrap.[4]

Although the Waltons also built the *Glenada* at Magnetawan in 1904, by then Sam Best had gone on to become the Crown lands agent at Magnetawan.[5] This career change would turn out to be a wise decision on the part of Best, for just a few years later in 1910, tote roads (those rough roads built by the logging companies so they could access their camps and clearings and also used by early settlers) from Burk's Falls to Magnetawan were beginning to cut into the

By the turn of the 20th century, tourism was at an all-time high. One of the most popular attractions was the trip down the Magnetawan River by steamer. This photograph shows the *Glenada* as she steams along Lake Cecebe. Built in 1904, her home "port" was Burk's Falls.

Photograph from Ted Bunt Collection, Burk's Falls and District Museum

steamboat trade. Arthur Walton's family, including his wife Rebekah, his niece and nephew Nellie and Ernest Sawyer, Arthur's brother Edgar, along with his wife Nellie and their daughters Margery, Ethel and Bertha, packed their belongings and headed for the Pickerel River in the fall of 1911. Arthur's other brother, William, along with his family was not far behind, arriving in Loring in January 1912. Also heading north were his son William and his wife Carolyn "Carrie," sons Leith "Bun," Merrill and Dob, and daughter Daisy.[6] Unfortunately by the end of the 1920s, history was to repeat itself. Trunk roads, upgraded tote roads, were being pushed through towards the isolated northern communities, and the Pickerel River, like the Magnetawan before it, lost its importance as a transportation corridor.

During the early years of settlement, Loring and Port Loring were both referred to as just Loring. When "Port Loring" came up in a conversation, it was generally known as "Down at the Lake" Wauquimakog (Wilson) Lake meaning "Lake surrounded by hardwood bush." But when the first post office opened July 17, 1922, the name Port Loring became official. Cecil Kidd was the first postmaster, and Ed Forsyth, the postmaster at Loring, came down to the port to assist him with the mail. In those early days the mail came in three times a week, in one day and out the next. During the winter it was an entirely different story. Mail came in whenever it got there, sometimes taking as long as a week to make the return trip. Cecil Kidd would run the post office at Port Loring until June 29, 1937.[7]

Introduction 15

The *Armour* travelled on the Magnetawan River as far as Ahmic Harbour. The ship was built in the winter of 1906, right at the wharf in Burk's Falls. George Strickland was listed as the shipbuilder. One of the largest steamships on the river, her estimated length was ninety feet, with a gross tonnage of 191 tons. The popular boat was often the setting for picnics and high tea. This photo is believed to have been taken during the 1908 shipping season.

River travel for the *Armour* meant going past the Midlothian Bridge, west of Burk's Falls. For many years Andrew Miller operated the hand crank to "swing" the bridge. Today, a modern two-lane stationary bridge replaces the historic structure. Fortunately, a section of the heritage bridge including the swing mechanism was salvaged and has a new home at the Burk's Falls and District Museum.

Port Loring was like most frontier towns of the time. Some inhabitants were a little more colourful than the rest and "The Port," as it was known by the local people, was no different. Take for instance Johnny Kyle and the brothers, Tom and Johnny Guthrie. Tom Guthrie was a carpenter by trade while his brother owned a mica mine further north on Caribou Lake. Although it wasn't until the First World War that the demand for mica reached an all-time high, as one of the first miners at Caribou, Johnny Guthrie managed to make a small fortune.

During the early years on the way to Loring was a sixteen-room hotel called the Fairview. It was situated at the "Y" in the road, near the log home of Robert George and his wife Mary Lucy (Davis) Brook. Whether Tom Guthrie actually built it is not known for sure, but the rumour was that he left the hotel to Johnny Kyle in his will. When Tom drowned in 1899, Johnny Kyle took it over. It then became known as the Red Hotel and was the favourite stopping place of lumberjacks and a Dr. Harcourt. Kyle is said to have kept a bear tied up at the hotel to attract customers.

Some of the people who worked at the Red Hotel included Kate, Maggie and Bridget Cain, John and Daniel Ennis, Richard Thorpe, Jacob Ratz, William Kyle, Fred Fleming and Bill and Florence Clapperton. A Miss Nickerson is reported to actually have lived at the hotel for several years to look after the rooms. One week's board at the hotel was $3 and meals were 25 cents. To feed the hotel guests, Johnny Kyle could get a whole lamb for $2.50, while a pig cost him $7. He paid $88.40 for a barrel of whisky and $31.05 for nine gallons of gin. The liquor was transported to the hotel by wagon and on more than one occasion the shipments would arrive late and be left outside overnight. Since it was quite easy to drill holes in the barrels to get a free drink, it didn't surprise Johnny one bit to find a pool of whisky on the ground and a drunk passed out under the wagon whenever he went out in the morning to check on his shipment. Sometimes the drunk was the teamster, sometimes it would be one of the locals. Kyle's hotel business lasted until 1913.[8] An enterprising man, he also had the stagecoach run in the early 1900s, carrying both mail and passengers. The mail was delivered along the way and horses were changed in Golden Valley.

But what was it like, when the territory was opened up to settlement, for the men who went into the forests to cut down what was left of the white pine after the original group of lumberman (including J.R. Booth) had clear-cut the north? And for the settlers that trekked across the district behind them with only the lumberjack's blazed trails as their guide? *Almaguin Chronicles: Memories of the Past* will, in part, take a closer look at how the lumbering industry and the people involved in it helped spread settlement through some of the "wildest" sections of the Parry Sound District.

There is no arguing that the lumbermen of the late 19th and early 20th century were a close-knit group despite the rivalry generated by the timber licences. And interestingly, the lumber fraternity represented a cross-section of society from both sides of the border. On the Canadian side, the Midland area was the home port for several notable lumbermen in the Parry Sound District, including Manley Chew and his brother and James Playfair. In 1875, the Chew brothers built a grist and lumber mill at Methodist Point in Midland, while Toronto-born Playfair was to head up a local consortium that eventually expanded Midland's lumber operations into shipping

As can been seen by this early postcard entitled "Making a Living in Burk's Falls, Canada," life was anything but easy. The driver is Bill McConnell and he is transporting a load of tanbark to the Magnetawan River Tannery Company that originally was located where the Highway #11 bypass now is. To get to the tannery, McConnell used the tote road that is now Highway #520. The tannery operated from 1894 to 1922. On the other side of the river is the Armstrong Boarding House, with Dr. M.A. Wittick's home seen high on the hill on the right.

Courtesy of Burk's Falls and District Museum

and grain handling. Both the Chew brothers and Playfair would become instrumental in the development—and eventual collapse—of the lumber industry in the area around Lost Channel. Although Manley Chew was elected as Liberal MPP for Simcoe East in 1908, almost nothing is known of his brother.[9] As for James Playfair, ten years later in 1918, he would purchase the Manley Chew home on Bay Street in Midland, and donate it to the town as the new hospital site, to be known as St. Andrew's. In turn, Playfair's wife, the past president of the hospital auxiliary, donated the house next door for a nurses' residence.[10] James Playfair was not only a lumberman, but an entrepreneur, willing to take risks that would lead to numerous fortunes. Sadly, his final venture at Lost Channel, which was the purchase of John Schroeder's mill with partner George Bruce, would lead to financial ruin and the eventual death of both men.

Although the Schroeder Mills and Timber Company of Milwaukee, Wisconsin, arrived in Parry Sound District at the tail end of the golden age of logging, Schroeder made the best of it. Not only did he manage to acquire timber holdings in a number of north-end townships, he was also successful in his bid for a timber licence in the provincial government lottery of 1910 that gave him ownership of the last stand of virgin pine in the region. His biggest coup, however,

Two views of the building of an early dam across the Pickerel River. The construction of dams on rivers made it possible to float logs from the camps far upstream to the navigable waters of Kidd's Landing. The stream of water had to be clear of obstacles, and dams were built to hold enough water to cover the shallows and rapids. Information on the date or at what section of the Pickerel River the dam construction took place was not available.

was the hostile takeover of the mill at Lost Channel in 1919, which included the Key Valley Railway, a spur line that linked Lost Channel to Pakesley on the CPR, and additional timber limits. Schroeder would later sell the mill to Playfair in 1926 and move on.

The Pickerel River set the stage for the last great run on the district's white pine, and not just by lumbermen like Playfair, Bruce and Schroeder. As a waterway, the system was navigable for pointer boats and small steam tugs from Georgian Bay to Kidd's Landing on Squaw Lake, located a few miles inland, northwest of Lost Channel. However, from here eastward along the Pickerel River system to Dollars Lake (immediately north of Lost Channel), the numerous rapids made the river waters boil. Dollars Lake was the largest lake on the Pickerel River system, and early loggers built a dam at the foot of the lake to maintain an adequate supply of water flowing over the rapids, thus allowing logs to float above them. Both the lake and the dam were named after two lumberjack brothers—Walter and John Melville Dollar. To their fellow loggers, the duo apparently so enjoyed the life, as the story goes, that they turned to contracting river drives and buying up timber stands along the way. Many an old-timer will reflect that there was something about a log drive that compelled the river men to dig out their caulked boots and check the rows of steel spikes to ensure that not one was missing, loose or bent. Although John Dollar became part of the Ontario Lumber Company (OLC) consortium for a while, there is no mention of his brother's involvement in the business. For certain, the work may have been hard, but it was exciting and the men were free. It is believed that once John Dollar left the OLC at Georgian Bay, he continued on with the contracts, driving great booms of logs to Detroit and Chicago.[11]

Photograph from Ted Bunt Collection, Burk's Falls and District Museum

Tugboats were essential in transporting log booms to the various sawmills along the Magnetawan River. Here the *Theresa* is seen leaving Marsden's Landing with her log boom. The small shanty on the left was built on a scow and provided temporary sleeping quarters for the river drivers.

One of the first lumber companies to acquire timber rights in the Loring area was Turner Lumber of North Bay. With only a long winding river and no network of passable roads, getting the logs to a mill was a challenge. Fortunately, there was a solution. Between the years 1890 and 1900, the company brought a steam alligator called *The Traveller*, built by West & Peachey of Simcoe, Ontario,[12] to tow logs from the Long Slide to Dollars Dam on the Pickerel River. One may ask, what is a steam alligator? Actually a boat, the vessel was large and square-ended, about twelve feet wide and twenty-four feet long. It's been said that the steam blowing out of the stack "devoured" four-foot pieces of wood at an astounding rate. But it was the only way to generate enough power to drive the side paddlewheels and turn the drum that wound the mile-long, one-inch-diameter steel cable. The process was long and arduous. The alligator would steam forward about a mile, and then the river drivers would anchor the cable, then hook the cable end onto a boom of logs. The cable would be wound up on the alligator's winch. This process was repeated until the boom reached its destination. When the alligator came to a dam, being flat bottomed, it was winched around the dam on land by its own cable. If one searches carefully, traces of old alligator trails can still be found at Dollars and other dams along the Pickerel River.[13]

A Settler's Story: The Founding of Burk's Falls

What was it about the northern backwoods that motivated so many in the late 19th century to leave the familiarity of established towns and cities of southern Ontario behind? Certainly, the availability of free land grants in Parry Sound/Muskoka, glowingly reported on by newspapers of the time, did much to promote the region. The appeal continued even when it became all too apparent that these free grants, under the Ontario Free Grants & Homestead Act of 1868, were routinely suspended by the government from time to time, unannounced and without explanation.[1] But being lured by the prospects of wealth and the chance to create something of one's very own in the wilderness seemed to be all the spirited pioneer needed by way of an incentive.

By the late 1870s it appeared nothing would stop the flow of people to the region hugging the shore of eastern Georgian Bay (originally referred to as the Magnetawan District).[2] During lapses in the free grant lands, a number of settlers turned to purchasing vacant lands, often paying 70 cents per acre, in cash, or $1 on time.[3] Then there were the squatters who, upon arriving in the territory, simply cleared a small patch of land and set up housekeeping. However, when in effect, the free land grant policy made a handsome offer—200 acres for every man with children under the age of eighteen, with the provision of an additional 100 acres at 50 cents an acre to be paid in cash. Each member of his family over the age of eighteen would also qualify for a grant of 100 acres. Conditions tied to the free grants required the settler to remain on the property for six months of the year. If the minimum amount of two acres of land were cleared annually for a period of five years, the deed would then be issued at the end of the fifth year. As an added incentive, the Homestead Law made the provision that if the original settler or his heirs remained on the claim it could not be seized for debt until after twenty years had lapsed.[4]

However, the daunting task of homesteading was further complicated by the government restrictions on the disposal of the timber growing on this land being cleared "for purposes of settlement," particularly on the removal of pine. Although stands of maple and beech are seldom noted in early records, there certainly was plenty of pine and birch. In its attempts to prevent speculators from clear-cutting, the free lands policy decreed that the settler would pay the government 75 cents for every thousand feet of pine if he sold it.

This was viewed as an undue hardship by many who supported settlement in the new territory, including temperance man Thomas McMurray, Parry Sound's first newspaper publisher. McMurray argued that unless there was navigable water close by, the fee to the government took away the settler's profits, as he could not afford to draw the logs to any market. He and his supporters pointed out that the only means left to the settler clearing his property, was to set fire to the trees.[5] In 1869 alone, one year after the Free Grant Lands Act came into effect, thousands of dollars worth of timber being cleared in Parry Sound went up in smoke. Despite McMurray's fierce lobbying efforts, government agents did little to ease the restrictions. However, for the more enterprising pioneers who happened on acreage with water access, untold riches awaited them. The lumbering business was now booming with the influx of new settlers. To meet the increased demand for building materials, so many sawmills were set up between Bracebridge and North Bay that they were actually within hearing distance of each other.[6] But, for as many pioneers who did prosper, there was an almost equal number who did not. Countless individuals venturing into new territory encountered hostile conditions, not the least of which were created by settlers who knew nothing of farming.[7] Captivated by what they read in the newspapers, an untold number of families arranged for a one-way ticket north. It wasn't long after all the timber was cleared and the stumps removed, that the realization sunk in—there was little left of their land other than sand and rock. If the settler didn't die of starvation, he certainly suffered almost everything else. Each had to come to grips with the fact that the "best" land the new territory could offer them was a reddish sandy soil capable of sustaining only a meagre crop of turnips, or potatoes at best. As for the water supply, in many areas it was a tea-stained colour, embittered by balsam and pine roots. An article that appeared in a St. Mary's, Ontario, newspaper during the late 1870s, summed up the plight of the ill-prepared settler in these words: "The residents are chiefly emigrants from English cities, who know nothing of farming…it is pitiable to see the shifts they are put to in some cases—the broken-heartedness visible upon their features, and the utter wretchedness of their lives. In many cases the remnants of luxury add to a kind of ghastly significance to the scene—silk dresses, faded and torn—the remnants of fine carpets, and other mementoes of an easy and comfortable existence among friends in the old country."[8]

By the mid-1870s, the Ontario Free Grants & Homestead Act had new territory to conquer and the second wave of settlers, including David Francis Burk of Oshawa, was pushing its way further and further north past Huntsville. Their goal was to stake land claims.[9] Frank, as his family and friends fondly called him, first learned of the Muskokas as a teenager. His father, David Burk Sr., who by 1865 was a successful farmer as well as holding the office of reeve of Oshawa, took a trip north that year with some of his associates.[10] Upon the senior Burk's return, nightly tales of adventure fairly rang off the walls of the family parlour. The stories were to leave a lasting impression on the young teenager, for nine years later Frank was to embark on his own trip, one that took him into virgin territory. The year was now 1874 and Frank was just twenty-four. Reaching the banks of the Magnetawan River late in the season, the young man from Oshawa became the first white

A Settler's Story

After he settled on his land claim, David Francis Burk, or Frank as he was fondly referred to by family and friends, built his first log home in 1876. The original Burk homestead is aptly described in a *Toronto Mail* article of July 30, 1892, as being "20 by 22 feet." Pictured here is a copy of a postcard, showing the Burk cabin at the north end of town between Ontario and Syples streets.

man to view the magnificent falls.[11] So enchanted by what he saw, he ended up staking his claim right then and there. Although Frank cleared two acres of land just below the junction of the south branch of the river, where it veered off to the west, it wasn't until the following year that he returned with his family in tow.[12] In order to cross the falls, a narrow wooden footbridge was needed, so Frank set about to build one. It is said that Frank carried the nails on his back all the way from Katrine.

By 1876 Frank Burk had settled on his land claim on the banks of the Magnetawan River, along with his wife Alice and their young daughter Ida. By constructing a log cabin here, Frank acquired the distinction of being the first white settler to take up permanent residence in the area.[13] The original Burk homestead was aptly described in a *Toronto Mail* article of July 30, 1892, as being:

> 20 by 22 feet in dimensions, roofed with basswood troughs, logs of that material split in two, hollowed out, and laid scoop side upwards close together, with an

inverted one covering each joint. The floor of the primitive domicile was, moreover, of balsam poles, smoothed with an adze after being pinned down, and in blocking out the door and window frames the only cutting instrument used was an axe.

When he later replaced his shanty with a large, two-and-a-half storey frame house, Frank proudly christened it the Burk House. By this time the Burk family had grown to include a son Walter, and another daughter, Mabel. As the stream of settlers continued to flow into the area, the Burk House became more than just a home for the growing family. It became the centre of a growing community as well, serving as a hotel, a post office, general store and a house of worship. And little wonder—the Burk House, with its commanding view of the Magnetawan River and the falls, provided its guests with every creature comfort available at the time. As far as the residents were concerned, Frank Burk was both a genial and popular proprietor and landlord. And he was often spotted offering information to incoming tourists, on fishing, hunting and scenic excursions through the neighbourhood.[14]

Despite the settlement's lack of size, it made up for it in location. As a result, the community had a surprisingly large number of mercantile businesses, all vying to serve the "scene loving"

Most of Almaguin still had dirt roads when the automobile made its first appearance. This postcard shows the main street of Burk's Falls looking south. The large imposing building on the bottom right is the Sharpe Block, which housed businesses on the main floor and a concert hall upstairs. One of the most celebrated 19th-century artists to appear at the hall was the Mohawk poet Pauline Johnson of the Six Nations Reserve near Brantford, Ontario. In the early 1900s, she embarked on a series of reading tours, visiting many remote communities including Burk's Falls. As was the practice of the time, she presented her poetry reading as a stage performance.

Courtesy of Betty Caldwell, property of Burk's Falls and District Museum

In the early 1930s, the Sharpe Block continued to command an important corner of the business section of Burk's Falls. However, the structure was already beginning to deteriorate. Gone was the second-floor balcony and most of the decorative wooden fretwork. Still a popular stop for tourists and the travelling public, its shops carried a variety of goods. Eventually left to fall into ruin, the block was demolished in 1982. The site is now a parkette named in honour of former Parry Sound–Muskoka Conservative MP Stan Darling.

tourist. And those tourists certainly didn't need Frank's word on what was in store for them, if they happened to ponder on a tour along the Magnetawan River. All they had to do was look out of his hotel's windows. If they did happen to decide to take a trip along the river's forty miles of navigable water, they had their choice of two steamers belonging to the Muskoka and Georgian Bay Navigation Company—the *Wenonah* or the *Glen Rosa* (or *Glenrosa*). Offering a panoramic display of beautiful water scenery seldom equalled at the time, travel on the Magnetawan River took the tourists in a northwesterly direction through Lake Cecebe and the government lock at Magnetawan to "Ah-Mie" Lake and ending at "Ah-Mie" Harbour, known today as Ahmic Harbour. To make travel all the more convenient for these early tourists, the new Clifton House, located right on the village's main street, joined the Burk House in offering hospitality Both offered their hotel guests return-trip carriage service to the wharf as well as to the train station.

The fancy Clifton House was built by James Sharpe, who completed it in 1887, exactly two years after the railway had pushed through. Born in Haughton, England, James arrived in Canada in 1871 and soon settled in Muskoka District's Chaffey Township.[15] A few years later,

Top: Here the *Wanita* stops to pick up passengers along the Magnetawan River. Compact in size, she travelled the waters for many years as both steamer and tug, until catching fire at Ahmic Harbour in 1932. The ship's remains are said to rest at the bottom of the bay. ***Bottom:*** The *Armour* is seen entering the locks at the Village of Magnetawan in the early 1920s. The photograph shows that by this time the community had grown considerably, while just to the south of it, the majority of the little settlements along the Nipissing-Rosseau Colonization Road were slowly disappearing.

Sharpe arrived in Frank Burk's little settlement and immediately sensed its potential for growth. It wasn't long before Sharpe threw himself into assisting Burk in developing the community.[16]

However, with less than 700 inhabitants, Frank Burk's little settlement had little to distinguish it from other villages springing up in the new territory. The buildings were, for the most part, of wood. Only the brick courthouse and gaol erected in 1887, overlooking the Knight Bros. Sash and Door Factory, could be considered the one truly imposing public building in the settlement.

The gaoler at the time was William Wilson. Like most of the area's settlers, Wilson came to the community from southern Ontario—in his case from Lanark County. Born in Scotland in 1829, while still a young man he emigrated to Canada. Once in his newly adopted country, he married Janet Walhope Neptune McMillian, who also hailed from Scotland. Interestingly enough, while the name Walhope is an ancestral Scottish surname, the name "Neptune" comes from an entirely different source. The McMillians were onboard the *Neptune* as she was crossing the North Channel between Scotland and Ireland when Janet was born. As was the custom at the time, the captain made the request that the baby be named after his ship. Janet's parents granted the wish.[17]

Soon after William and Janet were married, they moved north to just outside Frank Burk's little settlement, and took up farming. However, once their two sons, James and John, were of age, the farm was turned over to them and the couple moved into town. With Wilson's becoming the gaoler, he also took on the role as the settlement's first undertaker. He is reputed to have quite often stayed overnight at the courthouse. In its 120-year history, the courthouse, which still stands, has served as the Continuation School, the Vic Fell Memorial Branch 405 of the Royal Canadian Legion and currently as a private home.

It has been said that when the settlement was incorporated in 1890, Frank Burk and another early settler by the name of Henry Knight flipped a coin to choose an official name for both the community and the falls. Seemingly Burk won the bet as the name became Burk's Falls. However, Henry (known as Harry) and his brother Walter Knight were already at work harnessing the power of the falls for their sawmill. In its heyday, the Knight Bros. Sash and Door Factory was the largest employer in the area and eventually became the largest manufacturers of tongue and groove flooring in the British Empire. James Sharpe greatly assisted the growth of the business as he had been largely responsible for getting a rail line built down to the factory. This spur line became known as the Magnetawan River Railway. However, despite the success of the Clifton House, in 1889, Sharpe sold it to Fred Brasher, then turned his attentions to politics. A year later James Sharpe ran for reeve of the newly incorporated Burk's Falls—and won.[18] Continuing with his political aspirations, Sharpe entered the race to become the Liberal MPP for Parry Sound District in 1891, and won the seat with ease.

Frank Burk was to die on June 13, 1901, in the community he founded and where he is buried. His only son, Walter, passed away the following year at the age of twenty-four—the same age as his father had been when he first spotted the falls. Walter is buried next to his father in the Burk's Falls Cemetery.[19] As for Frank's widow Alice, she ran the Burk House for a couple of years

Top: Prior to the turn of the 20th century, grading the hill at the north end of Burk's Falls was done with teams of horses. It was an arduous task during frontier days, with the mud roads and wooden sidewalks. On the left near the crest of the hill is the Clifton House, built in 1887 on the site of the former H.W. Trimmer House. *Bottom*: With Burk's Falls continuing its growth into the 20th century, more and more businesses were opening up. This photograph of 1911 shows the inside of the bakeshop owned by the Glenney family. The little girl standing on the stool is believed to be Lila Hillis. In subsequent years the bakeshop became the home of the T.C. Dempster family, who for many years owned the funeral parlour next door.

Top: Combining several businesses under one roof was one way to ensure a livelihood in the early days of settlement. Here, R.J. Thorpe operated not only a funeral parlour but a furniture store as well. During the winter months the hearse was moved about by a sled, with the horses appropriately shrouded in black. ***Bottom***: Aptly named the Cataract House, this popular hotel was located just above the falls in Burk's Falls. In 1885, there were three hotels in the little settlement: the Burk House, owned by D.F. Burk; Trimmer's Hotel, owned by H.W. Trimmer; and the Cataract House, operated by the Mulheron Bros. Lodgings could be had for as little as $1 a day but cost $2 at the Cataract House.

before selling out in 1906. She left Ontario with her daughters Mabel and Ida, and took the family to Zion City, Illinois. Unfortunately, both the Burk House and the Clifton House, along with the main business section of the village, burnt to the ground in the great fire of 1908.

In a number of historical publications, Frank's wife was always been referred to as Olive. But her death notice printed in the February 21, 1944, edition of the Illinois *Waukegan News Sun*, referred to her as Alice (Simpson) Burk, not Olive. Incidentally, Alice Burk passed away at the grand old age of 94. After setting foot in the United States, Alice and her daughters took up residence just outside Zion City where Mabel, then 39, married Richard Hendrichson, 51, in May of 1920. He died less than five years later. The widowed Mabel went on to enjoy a fifteen-year career at the nearby Glen Flora Country Club. According to newspaper clippings, her sister Ida, in the meantime, had married a John Johnson.

The countryside may have been rustic, but local fashion kept up with the times. This postcard from the early 20th century depicts a group of picnickers enjoying the view of the Magnetawan valley west of Burk's Falls. Note the elaborate hats worn by the women. It is most likely that this party of six had disembarked from one of the regular steamers on the Magnetawan River to hold their picnic on the shore.

Had Frank Burk's move north been entirely influenced by his father's tales of 1865 or was he simply following a long-established family tradition? In 1725, while still a youth, Frank's great-grandfather Francis Burk emigrated from Ireland to America. Then, almost seventy years later, his son John Burk, enticed by Ontario's original free land grant policies, uprooted his entire family from their home near the north branch of the Susquehanna River in upper New York State and moved to Upper Canada.[20] John Burk became one of the first United Empire Loyalist settlers to take up residence in Darlington Township (east of York) in October of 1794. After receiving his own land grant of four hundred acres in 1798, alongside the swift flowing Barber (Bowmanville) Creek, he proceeded over time to acquire over one thousand

The Magnetawan River and Lakes Steamboat Line's finest are lined up here at the Burk's Falls wharf, circa 1909. Leading the way is the massive *Armour*, built in 1906, followed by the *Wanita*, built in 1896, and the *Gravenhurst*, built in 1902. All three steamers operated on the Magnetawan River from the time of the ice break-up in spring to the freeze-up in the fall.

acres of land on which he built the community's first gristmill and first sawmill. By the 1820s there was also a store and an inn on the property. Although John Burk had prospered in a relatively short time, for some unknown reason, he left the Bowmanville area in 1818 and returned to New York State, leaving his family behind. Later, Burk's descendants were to inherit the massive property that in time would become Darlington Provincial Park and the site for the Darlington Generating Station.

Pioneer Adventures: The Arrival of the Train

By 1884 the Grand Trunk Railroad from Toronto to North Bay had reached as far north as Sundridge before running out of rail. It had taken almost thirteen years for the government to make up its mind to continue the railroad through the Free Grants Districts, and thus launch the golden age of railways in the north.[1] However, for one young teenager, the significance of the railway's arrival in Sundridge was on a more personal level and her excitement almost proved to be too much. It was something that she would remember for the rest of her life. At the age of fourteen, Emma Louise Anderson was to be the youngest among the first "passengers" on the freight train out of Sundridge heading back to Gravenhurst to pick up more rail.[2]

It was nothing short of pure luck for Emma that her family wound up on that southbound train. Under normal circumstances the trip to Gravenhurst would have been made by stagecoach since that was as far north as the train went in those days. Once there, anyone wanting to travel further south would catch a train. There is nothing on record to indicate how the Andersons managed to convince the engineer of their need to board his freight train. But with Emma's sister Mary having a husband (John Carter, whom she married in 1882), who owned one of the first general stores in Sundridge, it is possible that Mary was in a hurry to get to Toronto as quickly as possible to pick up dry goods. In the end, a deal was struck, with the women happily riding in the caboose (the train would have been travelling in reverse on the southbound trip back to Gravenhurst) while Emma's father and the rest of the rail crew settled themselves on a flatbed. Once in Gravenhurst, only Mary and her mother continued on to Toronto by regular train, while the rest of the family waited for their train to be loaded with rails for the trip back to Sundridge.[3]

Over the years Emma became quite daring for a woman—a rarity in the late 19th and early 20th centuries. She not only managed a ride on the first train leaving the settlement—and back again, but also in one of the first automobiles to actually attempt the trip north through to North Bay. She never married and lived to a ripe old age, outliving her parents, four brothers and one sister. Emma passed away at Eastholme Home for the Aged in Powassan on September 2, 1974, just days before her 103rd birthday.[4]

Looking more like a frontier town, by the 1920s Sundridge was well on its way to becoming a modern community, offering the convenience of gas pumps for the motoring public and paved sidewalks. The streets, however, were still dirt roads. The riders pictured here are most likely campers from Canada's first private girls' camp—the Glen Bernard Camp in Sundridge, founded by Mary S. Edgar in 1922. The camp continues to operate to this day.

It was during her 100th birthday celebrations held on the family homestead in Sundridge (now the site of Ten Gables Golf Inn) on August 29, 1971, that Emma was asked if she remembered what the village was like before the turn of the 20th century. She is reported to have laughed and said, "Oh, I don't know, but we had an awfully good time." Looking back at her life, she wasn't far off the mark. As to her longevity, Emma attributed her long life to being raised in a good home. She never smoked or drank but then back in her day, she'd say, "It wasn't fashionable for young women to do so."[5]

The daughter of William and Margaret (Milne) Anderson, Emma was born on the family homestead located in Huron County's community of Belmore, Howich Township, on September 9, 1871. It was only in her later years that Emma took time to reflect on her family's pioneer roots and wrote countless letters on the subject to her nephews.

Her father William, she would recall, was born in Ireland in 1823. He, along with his parents, three brothers and four sisters, emigrated to Canada in 1835, settling at Rice Lake near Peterborough. Emma's mother, Margaret, on the other hand, was born in Elora, Ontario, on August 25, 1838, just two years after her parents, John and Mary (Woir) Milne had emigrated from Scotland.[6] Four years after their arrival, the Milnes purchased a farm east of Fergus, Ontario, where the family lived until 1855. The next move was to Belmore where Emma's parents were to meet. After a brief courtship, they married on June 5, 1857, and settled on a 200-acre farm that had been purchased by William just the year before. But like numerous other settlers of the time, William Anderson was always keeping an eye out for better opportunities for his family. The move north was most likely prompted by the glowing reports on the area written in the letters that Margaret received from her brothers John and James. The Milne brothers had been drawn to Stirling Falls, south of what was to eventually become Sundridge, after John learned of the availability of land here under the Ontario Free Grants & Homestead Act. In 1877, he made the decision to leave Huron County and the Village of Ethel behind.[7]

The Move North

William and Margaret's first visit to the area came in the summer of 1879. Travelling by train to Gravenhurst, the Andersons, accompanied by their son Howard, age five, then switched to one of the regular steamers heading north from Gravenhurst to Bracebridge. From there a stagecoach took them as far as Port Sydney situated at the lower end of Mary Lake. The family had to rely on the steamers passing through the locks into Fairy Lake to get them to Huntsville. Another stagecoach took them from there as far as Burk's Falls. By now, travellers heading north out of Huntsville had an easier time of it as the provincial government had constructed permanent wooden bridges to span the Magnetawan River at both Katrine and Burk's Falls. Prior to 1879, crossing the river at Doe Bay in Katrine was over a makeshift bridge of flattened timber.[8]

However, in reaching Burk's Falls, the Andersons had been expecting to be met by a teamster they had arranged for ahead of time to take them on to Stirling Falls. In those days, settlers heading north of Burk's Falls relied heavily on the hiring of teamsters as a method of transportation. Unfortunately for the family, the teamster failed to show, leaving the Andersons with no choice but to walk the six miles north. With luggage in hand, they followed a trail that had been cut through the forest. But, they could count themselves among the lucky ones! When the first settlers came and were making their way to Sundridge, a fairly well-travelled route only went as far as Katrine. Anyone venturing to Burk's Falls and beyond had to follow the surveyors' lines or sometimes blaze their own trail when that line came to an end.[9] The Andersons were so hampered by excess luggage on this first journey that they were unable to carry their young child, so he walked as well. Howard would later reflect that the brutal trail conditions caused him to develop water on his left knee. It was something he would nurse for the next twenty-one years.[10]

In those early days, there were only two ways for settlers to reach Sundridge. One could choose the stagecoach from Rosseau that would take them along the Rosseau-Nipissing Colonization Road or follow the route north from Katrine. The colonization road went as far as Magnetawan. From there settlers had to travel eastward on foot along whatever trails the surveyors had blazed. It is interesting to note that the colonization road had been in use long before anyone caught sight of Stony Lake (now Lake Bernard). In fact, it wasn't until the period between 1876 and 1877 that

As the community continued to modernize, safety issues became a concern for the town fathers. With fires becoming all too frequent, brick-clad buildings were one solution. This postcard shows two of the first structures to be bricked over, including Sundridge's new post office, second building on the left.

Courtesy of Burk's Falls and District Museum

the area's first permanent settlers were to even venture as far east as the lake.[11] And on they came, banking on the expectations that the railway was coming their way.

During that memorable trip north in the summer of 1879, the Andersons were encouraged to join John Milne and his wife Eliza, on a walk through the forest to Stony Lake where Milne's old neighbour from Ethel, James Dunbar, had set up a sawmill at the head of the lake. Arriving in the area in 1876, Dunbar had immediately abandoned the carriage trade and had turned to lumbering.[12] Some historians feel that Dunbar should be recognized as the first settler in the community. However, there are others who point out that John Paget should receive the credit, as it was Paget who opened up the post office (1880) two years after he arrived. The village was to be called Sun Ridge, the name chosen to reflect a picture of a sunny ridge—the high land to the north of the community. Unfortunately, the mail stamp from Ottawa was printed Sundridge, and the name stuck.[13]

To get his visitors to Dunbar's sawmill, John Milne turned to brothers Pat and Jim Flynn who owned a rowboat, the intention being to cross the lake by boat. However, when the group reached the landing, to Pat's dismay, someone had stolen the oars! He assured them that he could use a paddle to navigate around the lake. As luck would have it, because of just the one paddle and with the boat heavily loaded with people, Pat could venture only as far as Archie Menzies Landing.[14] William Anderson certainly didn't need to go any further, for he discovered a delightful spring of cold water cutting through the property. He also observed a beautiful sugar bush, but what completely took his breath away was the spectacular view of the lake. With the rumours spreading fast that the railway survey west of Stony Lake was about to be approved, William Anderson saw his opportunity. He wanted this parcel of land and, when approached, Archie Menzies, the settler who owned the land, agreed to sell the 200-acre property—lots 18, 19 and 20 on the 8th Concession, Strong Township.

Despite the primitive conditions awaiting them, William and Margaret made plans to return north as soon as possible. So in the winter of 1881, not just their son Howard, but also his sisters Mary and Emma were to join them on the trip. Howard was later to recall that the family was detained in Orillia for two nights and one day because of a severe snowstorm. They eventually arrived in Sundridge by sleigh.[15] The Andersons promptly turned an existing log shanty on the Menzies property into their new home. Records show a few family members did make one last trip back to Belmore, including Emma's sister Mary, who in January of 1882 had married John Carter whom she had met there. It turned out to be the last family gathering at the old Huron County homestead. The following year the property was sold, and by the winter of 1884 the Carters had made the decision to join the rest of Mary's family in Sundridge. Tragically, the couple's infant daughter Effie, age thirteen months, took sick on the journey north and died in Huntsville. Her parents took the body with them to Sundridge where, on January 5, 1884, the day of the Carter's second wedding anniversary, Effie was buried.[16]

That same winter William Anderson purchased a second piece of property, a 100-acre parcel of land from William Lang that comprised of lot 21, Concession 10, in Strong Township. Six years later a large brick house was built for the family at this location. Ben McDermott has been listed as the builder, with the bricklayer identified by the last name of Glover and the inside plasterer as Bagshaw. The home still stands today as the Steirerhut Restaurant on Highway #11 S.[17] But just two years prior to William Anderson's purchase of the Lang property, his in-laws, the Milnes, had been busy establishing themselves in Stirling Falls. John Milne had finally gained title to his 100 acres on October 5, 1882, while James Milne had established the first gristmill in Stirling Falls, powered by water from Bernard Creek.[18] Ironically, it would be the arrival of the railway that would force the Milne clan to pull up stakes and move elsewhere. The Grand Trunk Railway bypassed Stirling Falls, choosing instead a route through the community just north of it—Sundridge—exactly what William Anderson had been counting on from that summer day back in 1879 when he first spotted his land.

With the Andersons firmly established in Sundridge and awaiting the arrival of the railway, James Milne decided to sell his gristmill and move further north to Powassan. His brother John, now fifty, opted to go south to Huntsville and open up a planing mill. The money for the Huntsville mill is reportedly to have come from John's mother, Mary, who had interests in a gristmill back in Ethel. However, a fire in 1883 destroyed the Huntsville business, and with it, John's desire to remain in the area. Both the family's home and the mill property were sold the same day in May 1893.[19] Packing up his family, he headed south, this time to Cleveland, Tennessee. It was here that John Milne opened up a chair factory just three months after his arrival. The business was so successful that John and Eliza made enough money to eventually return north to Burk's Falls. Their sons, Jack and Walter, were left to run the factory on their own.[20]

The Trip by Motor Car

Jack Milne, who had been left in charge of the chair factory, had more than just chairs on his mind. With the arrival of the 20th century came the automobile. And in August of 1905, Jack and his brother Walter, left Tennessee in a brand new Rambler powered by a two-cylinder, sixteen-hp engine, built by the Thomas B. Jeffery Company in Kenosha, Wisconsin. They were to pick up their cousin Emma, now living in Richmond Hill, for the trip north. Emma had informed her cousins that she had set her heart on driving the Rambler all the way to North Bay.

Unfortunately, the expedition ended rather badly for everyone concerned.[21] As Jack Milne was to recall, after picking up Emma, her brother Howard, who lived in Toronto, was wired to send her suitcase immediately to Sundridge. The first bit of bad luck for the trio was to occur

North Bay or Bust. Emma Anderson was one hardy pioneer and always ready for adventure. When her cousins the Milnes, Walter (left) and Jack, decided to drive their 1905 Rambler from Tennessee to North Bay, there was no doubt in anyone's mind that Emma would be coming along for the ride. Unfortunately, the terrain proved to be too much for the vehicle and Emma boarded the train in Huntsville for the remaining leg of the trip to Sundridge. The Rambler only made it as far as Burk's Falls.

when the Rambler crossed a broken culvert, just ten miles south of Gravenhurst. The motion of bouncing back and forth through the hole broke the Rambler's two rear springs. This, according to Jack, cut their speed to about four miles per hour. Thus, it took Walter, Jack and Emma almost three hours to cover the ten miles to Gravenhurst. Once there, the Rambler was taken to the local wagon shop where two wooden blocks were cut to fit in between the springs. It allowed the vehicle to go a little faster, about ten miles an hour. But what a trip on those rough roads! This was the first car to travel north of Bracebridge, and that in itself was an adventure.[22]

Seeing the road conditions for what they were, Walter wired on ahead to old friends Ab and Bill Hunter to meet them in Huntsville in order to help push the Rambler up the loose sand hills that surrounded the town. Emma, in the meantime, finding herself tired of the whole ordeal, boarded the train in Huntsville for the remaining trip to Sundridge. The brothers continued on to Burk's Falls but by this time, the Rambler had completely broken down. Since they couldn't repair it by themselves and in order to get their $800 deposit back from Canada Customs, the Milnes loaded the Rambler onto the southbound freight train and shipped it back to Tennessee. The $800 deposit, incidentally, had been required to allow the vehicle to cross the border into Canada.[23]

During those early years up to the death of the patriarch of the family, William Anderson Sr. in 1903, the entire family took a keen interest in the development of Sundridge, both before and following its incorporation as a village in 1889. One of Emma's brother, Albert, took up the mercantile business, selling everything from sewing machines to maple syrup evaporators. Another brother, William Edward Jr., or Edward as he was fondly known, established a sawmill on property that in later years under numerous ownerships was turned into a succession of tourist camps. John, another of her four brothers, took up farming on his parent's homestead where the Ten Gables Golf Inn is now.

After her father's death, Emma joined her brother Howard in Toronto, where, after graduating from the University of Toronto, he set up his dental practice at # 1 Carlton Street. Emma continued her independent life long after her brother died in 1963, living alone in the house she had shared with him until shortly after her 100th birthday.[24]

As for Emma's sister Mary and her husband John Carter, they left for the West Coast in the early 1900s. Carter sold his mercantile business to Joseph Edgar and his house on John Street in Sundridge to another family. Both buildings survive to this day. His general store enjoyed a long life under Edgar's ownership, in later years as Lang's General Store. It is now an employment resource centre with apartments upstairs.

Gold Rush

John Carter got his first taste of what the West had to offer when he caught gold rush fever along with brothers-in-law Edward, Howard and John Anderson, and old school chum, Bill Lane. They were to leave Sundridge on February 15, 1898, and head for the Klondike. Taking a tourist sleeper out to the coast, the men spent two days in Vancouver getting outfitted. One wise purchase made by them was four 4x8-foot tarpaulins that they anticipated could be used as sails if needed.[25] Hopping on a cattle boat, the *SS Danube,* which also carried a number of other passengers, they travelled up the coast between the mainland and Vancouver Island. From Queen Charlotte Sound, the *Danube* continued for many miles along a narrow channel until she reached Seymore Narrows. Unfortunately for the Sundridge party, this was the *Danube* captain's first trip and he misjudged the timing of the incoming tide. It was advancing far more quickly than he had anticipated, and four men were needed on the wheel just to keep the boat straight. As they headed into a bay, the swift tide turned the boat over on its side, dumping all the freight off the bow. Four heavily laden skids took away eighteen feet of railing. Crew and passengers spent two hours in the bay, waiting for the full tide. Once the boat was reversed out of the bay, the rest of the trip through the channel was in relatively calm water.[26]

The foursome eventually arrived at Skagway at around nine o'clock on the evening of March 1.[27] At the time Skagway was reported to be the most lawless town in America. The Andersons, Carter and Lane soon learned that it was not safe for a man to go out on the street alone, especially if he was carrying any money. The second night in Skagway, the men slept in a large room, with two of them on watch all night. Five days later the group headed out from Skagway Bay along the Dead Horse Trail to the summit of the White Pass. Howard was to recall in later years that it cost them five and a half cents a pound to have their gear freighted to White Pass, some twenty-two miles from Skagway. The gear, termed "Yukon outfits," cost between $500 and $700, and could weigh anywhere between 1,000 and 2,000 pounds.[28] As Howard Anderson would later reminisce, the group ended up working two of the most famous placer claims in the Klondike, the Bonanza and the Eldorado.

All four men eventually returned to Sundridge, and Howard went back to Toronto to resume his dentistry practice. In 1906, John Carter and Edward Anderson, along with their wives, moved out West. Settling in Vancouver, British Columbia, John established a real estate business while Edward started a salmon cannery at Quathiaski Cove across from the Campbell River and operated it until shortly before his death in 1940. A second salmon cannery was established at Blind Channel, where he also set up a shingle mill.[29]

Howard and Emma never completely severed their ties with the village they grew up in. In 1912, the brother and sister built the very first cottage on Lake Bernard on property that adjoined the former Layolomi Beach Inn. With no road access from the village, Howard purchased a twenty-six-foot cruiser that would become a familiar sight on the lake for many years.[30]

The Life of a River Driver

Clarence Brazier turned 100 years of age in August 2006. He is the first river driver I ever met, and most likely, will be the very last. His is an inspired life to say the least.

At his remarkable age, Clarence Brazier still takes pleasure in looking back and reflecting on his long life. One that began with learning to roll logs at the age of six, to that of a river driver when he was just fourteen. The only thing he never got around to doing was learning to read—that is, until he was well into his nineties. As Clarence explains it, he was a young boy attempting to leave his mark on the new frontier and learning to read didn't seem to matter all that much to him. Interestingly enough, by the time Clarence was born on August 28, 1906, the area's other "young pioneer," Emma Anderson, had already reached two milestones in her life, riding aboard a train before it was fully commissioned and driving an automobile. Clarence's early accomplishments would certainly turn out to be far less romantic, but a lot more dangerous.

The how and why to his life of illiteracy began simple enough. But learning to read at the age of ninety-three—well, that's an entirely different story. "I used to be ashamed to tell people that I didn't have an education. But I'm not ashamed anymore. I finally figured out it wasn't my fault that I couldn't go to school…after all these years I've now learned to look at the situation all differently." It all started back in the days when settlers were beginning to show an interest in the area just north of Muskoka, the region now called the Almaguin Highlands. Quite often properties would change hands several times before the pioneer found the ideal location to raise a family. Some would succeed while others failed miserably. Clarence was one of seven Brazier children growing up on what he called a "starvation farm." This was the Tom King homestead that, in the spring of 1904, Clarence's father, George Brazier, had purchased from a William Millen for the tidy sum of $450. A completely isolated property, it was located at the far end of North Whalley Lake Road near Doe Lake (now know as Whalley Lake), just north of the Village of Magnetawan.[1] Tom and his bride Annie Wilson had lived less than ten years on the property before they sold out to Millen in 1902 and moved to Croft Township, now part of the Municipality of Magnetawan. Tom was the eldest son of English market gardeners, John and Maria King, who had immigrated to Canada in 1875.

Whereas the King clan would achieve prosperity in their adopted country, the Braziers would not be so fortunate.[2] Clarence's parents George and his bride Frances Mae (Ward), were married in Bracebridge sometime around the turn of the 20th century, and eventually made their way north to Sundridge, where their eldest son Earl was born in 1902. George and Frances's families were among the untold hundreds of poor English immigrants who, back in the 1870s, came to Canada looking for a better life. The Braziers settled in southwestern Ontario where George was born on November 5, 1881, in the Town of Brantford situated along the Grand River. Clarence recalls being told that his mother's parents, John and Mary Ward, first settled in a place called Norland, south of Minden and that his mother was born on Valentine's Day, 1884. The Wards later moved to Burk's Falls where they lived in one of the Tannery houses (Highway #520) along the Magnetawan River. As for how his parents actually met, he can only shrug his shoulders.

What he does clearly remember to this day, was that his parents were dirt poor. By the time George Brazier purchased the farm near Magnetawan he was already heavily in debt. "My brother Earl was four years older than me and took up working on the water," Clarence recalled. "He didn't like to farm, not one bit. That's how when I was old enough, I got stuck with all the work!" And having to do the chores before school meant that by the time Clarence got there, he was

Pictured here is the Brazier family on their farm near Magnetawan prior to its being sold. In the front row (l–r) are sons Clarence, Don, Johnny, Wallace and Bill; in the back row (l–r) are George Brazier, son Earl, an unknown farm worker, daughter Ethel, and Frances Mae Brazier.

Courtesy of Doris Villemaire, daughter of Clarence Brazier

doggone tired. "I remember I was always tired. I'd fall asleep in school. When I got home, I was tired. So I finally figured why go to school? I wasn't getting anything out of it." Part of the problem, according to Clarence, was the fact that in order to get to school, he had to cross a mile of water and another two miles of land. Clarence's earliest encounter with education took place at the original Magnetawan Central School. which had been built in 1888. It was located next door to the present-day Magnetawan Community Centre and ultimately became a storage shed. In 2005, a fire burnt it to the ground.

But before he even got the chance to quit school, things would go from bad to worse. In 1911, when he was six years old, his father became permanently blinded, a victim of a farming accident. As Clarence remembers all too vividly, his father had been attempting to blast a drain in a rock crevice that was holding back the water to the farm. "He'd put in a stick of power, but the blackflies were so bad he couldn't see. Dad misjudged the timing and when he came back down to check on the fuse, it went off in his face. Both his eyes were blown from his head," he added, with a twist to his face. Any chance of him continuing his education promptly came to an end with this tragic accident. His younger brothers and one sister were luckier. As they reached school age they were able to attend the public school but for only four months of the year. Without Earl around and with the Brazier family continuing to grow, Clarence found himself as the man of the house. After his father's accident, any spare time he did have, he'd sneak off to the lake near the farm where he learned to roll logs. "I didn't have any other kids to play with, so I played with the logs. It was bad; we were really poor. But we

After George Brazier was blinded in a farming accident, he could never be left alone. Pictured here with George Brazier minding the sheep is his young son Wallace (extreme left, wearing hat). By this time a two-storey frame house had replaced the family's first home—the tiny cabin on the left. The frame house still stands today, although extremely altered in appearance.

never went hungry." Clarence developed a lifelong admiration for his mother, who worked tirelessly to ensure her children were fed.

In time Clarence received help with the chores from his younger brothers, William (Bill), Donald, Wallace, Johnny and from his sister Ethel, as they tried to make the work fun. But there was no fun to be had when the chores were nothing short of backbreaking work. During the summer months the Brazier children helped their mother pick berries from morning until dark for selling down in Toronto. The fruit was shipped south by train from Huntsville. Anything left over his mother preserved for the family. "We had food year-round. She would put as much as 500 quarts of raspberries, blueberries, strawberries and cranberries away," he said with some pride. By the age of eight Clarence resorted to making axe handles for a little extra bit of money. "I was selling them for 75 cents each. Factory handles were only 35 cents apiece, but I made mine flexible! And they sold," he smiled. "After all, I couldn't exactly leave home and find a job, I was only eight." To this very day he's never elaborated on just how he made the axe handles "flexible" as he put it. By the time he was twelve, Clarence was helping his mother run a hunt camp that attracted a number of rich Americans. The endeavour brought the family much needed cash. He also found work at a neighbour's farm as a chore boy. But it meant that after coming home at night he'd still have to tend to his own chores.

To make extra money, Frances Mae Brazier, pictured here second from right, guided hunting parties in the fall. The hunters are believed to be members of the Glover family.

George Brazier may have been blind, but he tried to stay active the best he could while the family toiled on the farm. Because the father could never be left alone, explained Clarence, when he went on occasion to purchase horses, he'd have to have someone along to lead him to the animals. "Then Dad would have to feel the horses all over, check the teeth and so on. He sure knew more about the horses than the fellows who were trying to sell them." Since there were no permanent roads at that time between Magnetawan and Burk's Falls, except for the logging company tote roads, the only other means of travel was on the river by steamboat. According to Clarence, his father was given a lifetime pass from "Bert" (Albert) Agar on the "old boat." "But he only used it [the pass] once or twice." He figured his dad was given the pass because Bert felt sorry for him. Unfortunately, ninety years later, Clarence no longer remembers the name of the "old boat."

Albert A. Agar was not only a well-known Burk's Falls merchant; he was also a prominent local shipowner. His fleet of steamboats included: the *Wanita*, built in Ahmic Harbour in 1896 and later renamed the *Cyclone*; the *Theresa*, built in 1900 at Rosseau Falls, and the *Gravenhurst*, built at her namesake town in 1902. Agar renamed the *Wanita* when he purchased her in 1899, but she burnt to the waterline while moored in Burk's Falls in December of 1911.[3] However, since the *Cyclone* was rebuilt as a tug and continued to operate on the Magnetawan River from 1913 onwards, the "old boat" Clarence remembers could very well have been the former *Wanita*.

The *Wanita* built in 1896 at Ahmic Harbour became a very popular little passenger boat after she was bought by Burk's Falls merchant Albert A. Agar. She is pictured here circa 1904 at Marsden's Landing. Although originally named the *Cyclone*, once the vessel was part of Agar's fleet he renamed her *Wanita*. She burned to the waterline in 1911 but was rebuilt as a tug in 1913.

Despite Frances Brazier's best efforts, the family continued to struggle to make ends meet. "After the accident my brother Earl kept passing a little money home, just to keep away from home. He sure had a system," recalled Clarence. But it wasn't all that many years later before he would follow in his brother's footsteps.

A setback for the family came during the 1918 influenza epidemic that swept through the district. Clarence and his brother Johnny both became seriously ill. Johnny, just four years of age, recovered, but was left without hearing and the capacity for speech. Clarence was luckier, winding up with scarred lungs and a body many pounds lighter. Sadly, his brother would die a few years later from a ruptured appendix while in a Belleville institution. Johnny Brazier was just seven. How many children in the area died as a result of the influenza epidemic? The names are now lost in the past. When asked if he remembers, "Most of the families around us had six children; there were six in the Milnes' family. Some had four children. Don't remember how many of them died. There were some."

But, in 1920, things brightened up considerably for Clarence when two fellows he knew from the Sundridge area offered to help him get a job with a local logging crew. They accomplished the feat by lying about Clarence's age. The company walking-boss stated that at fourteen he was too young to be hired on. If he was sixteen, well, okay. "Jack Russell and Henry Walsh vouched for me. They signed the papers, swearing I was sixteen," smiled Clarence. "There was no crime in it. They knew my father was blind. They knew I had to work."

Built in 1900 at Rosseau Falls, the *Theresa* was purchased by Albert A. Agar and became part of his fleet—the Magnetawan River and Lakes Steamboat Line. It wasn't until 1919 that the *Theresa* became a tugboat. Here, in her new life as a tug, she is pictured with a group of river drivers.

And work he did. At first, it was for a number of local enterprises. Among them were the Canada Pine Lumber Company in Kearney and Ted Hope's company in Parry Sound. Winter camps were usually set up in Ahmic Harbour, giving him the opportunity on occasion, to visit his grandparents in Burk's Falls. Eventually, Clarence went to work for Moore Lumber in Algonquin Park and remained with the company for two winters. By 1926 he'd left the area completely and found himself a job with the Grant and Dunn lumber company in Latchford, running logs down the Montreal River from Gogama to the mills in Latchford north of Temagami on the Montreal River. That same year his only sister Ethel would die of spinal meningitis, but he could not return for the funeral. "I just got the job, it took all the money I had to get up there. And all I could do was go to work," said Clarence. To this day a small quiver remains in his voice as he speaks of his sister's death. But, as he was being paid 50 cents a day as a driver while a grown man's wages were $1, he had little choice in the matter. He needed the money. Clarence later worked for a short time on the jack-ladder. "That's what takes the logs up from the boom to the sawmill," he explained. He became so skilled at his job, the walking bosses only gave him the best men to work with. By the age of twenty Clarence was a first-class river driver.

Pictured here, Clarence Brazier (with moustache) is with his uncles Aurele Boudreau (left) and Joe Boudreau, along with the family horses, Prince and Polly. By now Clarence was a full-fledged lumberman.

When telling stories of his days as a river driver, he remembers them as though they happened only yesterday—not eighty or more years ago. According to Clarence, when he first started out most waterways in the Parry Sound and North Bay areas were still in full use, transporting logs to the various mills. Between 1900 and 1920, there were seven major lumber mills in operation in the Nipissing Passageway alone. The output from these mills was between 25,000 to 50,000 board feet of lumber a day.[4]

And for the river drivers who were responsible for getting the logs to these mills, "some days were better than others. When the wind was good, the crews could work as much as 16 to 20 hours a day," explained Clarence. But when the wind was bad or it rained, the crews were forced to stay in camp all day. Sometimes it was for days at a time. It was a situation loggers had a tough time getting used to. The effect on men with nothing to do was particularly noticeable on Sundays, normally the only day off for the men. "With so much time on their hands, the men would start thinking and worrying about the home life they'd left behind so many months before," continued Clarence. "On Sundays, everybody in camp had something to worry about. Add a week of bad weather on top of it, the men would get mighty lonesome and then start quitting." When he first walked into the Canada Pine Lumber Camp, he spotted six fellows coming out. "The turnover was terrific," he recalled. To keep the men occupied, Clarence, along with his old friends, drivers Jack Russell and Henry Welsh, came up with the idea of starting an entertainment troupe. "We had tricks, stories and square dancing," he laughed. "It sure kept the spirits up." Clarence called the dances and there was usually someone who had a guitar or accordion to provide the music. As for the women, the dance sets were arranged by finding four "volunteers" to play the part of the girls. They would then dress up by wrapping towels around their waists.

As a result of entertaining the men on weekends—Saturday nights and a bit earlier on Sundays—the turnover of men dropped by over 50 percent. And the payback to Clarence and his partners was huge. Clarence, Jack and Henry were paid a bonus of $15 a month each, for three months. "The Canada Pine Lumber Company was glad to pay us," says Clarence. "They didn't lose as many men." And the bonus was on top of the wages, which were just $35 a month. There was lots of fun, too, in entertaining," he smiled. In fact, he liked it so much he continued to sing songs and entertain the men as he went from logging camp to logging camp.

During the seven years Brazier worked for the famous lumber baron, J.R. Booth, on his log drives down the Montreal River, he estimates about 20 percent of the pulp sunk. "I went down a couple of times with the pulp, but I was a good swimmer," he said. River drives in general come to an end in what's usually a really big lake. The logs are loose at this point and the crews have to boom the logs as they came into the lake. Sometimes the fellows would put the booms on the ice; sometimes they'd just be left in the water. "Then in the summer we'd tow the booms to the other end of the lake where the river goes out," explained Clarence. To prevent jams and bottlenecks from occurring, the drivers would have to get in among the logs to direct them into the river currents. It wasn't until he worked the Wild Cat Rapids up from Georgian Bay that it finally dawned on him just how dangerous this work could be.

"It happened with me personally. I remember it pretty well," said Clarence. "I had this partner named Earl Molten. A good river driver. They [the walking bosses] gave me the best they had. We'd been feeding the logs out of the lake into the river, been at it from 7:00 to 10:00 in the morning, and we wasn't watching what we were doing. All of a sudden we realized we were taking the stream ourselves. There was nothing we could do. We went over the dam." He explained that they were in what was called a twenty-two-foot pointer boat that normally accompanied the log drives and the vessel hit hard on the rocks below the dam. Badly damaged, the boat was dragged by the current over the second set of falls, causing the vessel to break in two. "I was hanging on to the one end of the boat; Earl was in the other. We were carried about another 1,000 feet, floating among the logs when all of a sudden Earl said, 'I'm going to make it for sure.' He jumped in and swam for it. Now Earl was a good swimmer, but he didn't get very far."

Clarence can still remember what happened next. A log came at Earl from behind him, and there was nothing Clarence could do to warn him. Earl had been swimming along one log, when another one floating in a vertical position, hit him in the head, sending him under. "He never saw it coming." Determined to cling to his half-boat, or he'd drown as well, Clarence drifted down the river along with the logs for about half a mile until a creek came into view. There were trees with overhanging branches and he climbed out hand over hand to shore, until he could get his feet under him. "The whole ordeal took me five hours. Then I strolled back into camp at around 3:00 in the afternoon after fighting my way back," he said with some pride. "The rest of the camp, they couldn't believe it when they seen me. Everybody was a yelling and a screaming. I've had lots of tests during my life. This was just one of them."

Death wasn't an uncommon occurrence among the river drivers. Unlike Clarence and Earl, there were many men hired on as drivers who couldn't swim a stroke.[5] And those with no known relatives or home addresses were given the rough burial of the lumber camps. According to Clarence, the burial went something like this: "They took them [drivers] in their blankets and dug a hole near a big shade tree. Then they'd roll the dead in their blankets and take off their boots. Big, seven-inch spikes were driven through the heel of the boot into the tree. This was their headstone." Earl Molton's headstone was a pair of boots along the Wild Cat Rapids. "I know people who told me that for years those boots stayed there. One fellow told me that even though the tree had eventually died, the boots were still there."

Clarence Brazier was now ready to leave the lumbering business and in the years following his river driver's job, he did everything from peddling milk, to door-to-door sales, a stint as a prison guard at the old Don Jail in Toronto and finally, he tried his hand at mining. The last time he was to see his grandparents, John and Mary Ward, was in 1928 (Clarence remembers his grandfather died at age eighty, but doesn't recollect the year of his death). As for his parents, according to Clarence, after his younger brothers were old enough to leave the farm, times became so tough that his father sold the property sometime between 1926 and 1928. The farm was acquired by Jack Sarares.[6] After the sale his mother had no choice but to go out and find work. Florence Mae was able to get a job as a cook on the railway (Ontario Northland) and eventually wound up in Timmins, where she was later reunited with Clarence and her eldest son, Earl. Florence would die in Timmins on September 5, 1982, at the age of ninety-eight, surrounded by her sons and granddaughters.

George Brazier, on the other hand, had no interest in moving. As Clarence remembers it, after the farm was sold, his father went and boarded with a Magnetawan family, Bill Harrison and his daughter Ada. The Harrisons had taken up lodgings in what was once the North Star Hotel and had room to spare.[7] Located where the Magnetawan Seniors' Friendship Centre now sits, the hotel, built circa 1890, was sold sometime after the turn of the 20th century to Thomas Hicks, who quickly turned it into a rental property. Members of the Joe Dickie family were Hicks's other tenants. According to Clarence, his family and the Harrisons had come to know each other through worship at the Plymouth Brethren Church in Chapman Township. Although his father rarely attended church, Clarence recalled that his mother went quite often and Bill Harrison was a member of the congregation. George eventually went to live in South River, where he passed away in June of 1947 at the age of sixty-six. Clarence made the trip south for the funeral. As he put it, he hadn't seen his father in years. As for the old North Star Hotel, it burned to the ground in 1965.[8]

At the time of his father's death, Clarence had already been married for thirteen years. After leaving the Parry Sound area, his first job was in Sudbury, delivering milk. However, when the Great Depression hit in the 1930s, it meant a resurgence in the demand for nickel and Clarence, now in his mid-twenties, was lucky enough to be hired on as a security police officer at the Coniston Smelter. But as he explains, his employment after this would always be short-lived. The reason? Although he had an uncanny knack for landing jobs, he couldn't hang on to them for long, because he couldn't fill out any of the forms. It was finally beginning to dawn on Clarence that he couldn't let on to anyone that he couldn't read. There would be a couple of more jobs, including ones that took Clarence to southern Ontario before he decided he'd had enough and returned to the north. After taking a job at the McIntyre Mine for 53 cents an hour, something quite unexpected happened. He fell in love.

Clarence met Angela Boudreau in 1932 when she was only fourteen years of age. He was twenty-six. Angela's early years had been spent in New Brunswick, before her parents Victor and Regina decided to take the train to Timmins—with their seven children in tow. Up until this time, Angela's life had been anything but easy. At the age of twelve she stopped going to school because she was needed at home to help her mother raise her younger siblings. Washing diapers and potty training became a way of life for Angela. Once in Timmins, another brother arrived—Armand. It was becoming a hopeless situation for her.

Although Victor Boudreau attempted to discourage the budding romance between his daughter and Clarence, it was Angela's mother who finally intervened. As Clarence fondly remembers, Regina helped the couple run away to get married in a church. The year was 1934 and Angela was now sixteen. Clarence built a three-room log cabin for them to live in, on what eventually became known as the Kam Kotia Road in Mountjoy Township, ten kilometres outside of Timmins. Clarence returned to logging for a while after he was married, hauling timber for the various mines in the Timmins area. Knowing all too well the dangers of mining, he eventually turned to farming to support his family, just as his father had done before him.

And his work, like his mother's, would also turn out to be endless. For the first number of years, there was no electricity, no running water or plumbing in their tiny cabin. With only an outdoor privy for a bathroom, the family resorted to chamber pots during the winter. A wood stove provided the necessary heat, but it meant the wood had to be carried in on a daily basis. Sadly, the couple's first child, a son named Ron, died very young, but within the first nine years of marriage three more children would arrive in quick succession—all daughters, Pearl, Doris and then Janet. In 1943, a fourth daughter, Irene, was born, completing their family. Angela was a smart woman, according to Clarence. She not only sewed all their daughters' clothes, but also found time to plant and care for a vegetable garden as well. She even made soap and preserved jams, pickles and jellies in season.

Angela found time to finish her education by attending night school and learned how to type. Now anything that Clarence needed in writing, his wife would take care of. It was a perfect partnership. According to her daughter, Doris Villemaire, Angela always held education in high esteem and eventually sat on the local school board. During the 1960s, her mother actually joined the New Democratic Party (NDP) and even managed a trip to Ottawa. But by then the years of hard physical work had taken its toll on her. While still in her sixties, Angela became severely crippled with rheumatoid arthritis. Clarence

Reflecting back on his long life, Clarence Brazier maintained that his biggest accomplishment, besides his family, was finally learning to read at the age of 93. At age 100, Canada Post awarded him the 2006 National Literacy prize and turned him into a poster boy for literacy.

Photograph by Astrid Taim

was resolved to keep his beloved wife close to him, nursing her for the next twenty years. When she finally died on January 15, 1999, they had been married for sixty years.

Her death left a void in his life and Clarence, now ninety-three, suddenly realized he didn't want to leave the three-room cabin he'd shared with her for all those years. But he couldn't just fill the days with knitting the odd sock and chopping firewood. Then one day after the mailman had left, the idea came to him. Left with all that junk mail, he was determined to learn how to read it. According to his daughter Doris, it became a way out of loneliness for her father. Sensing what he was up to, during one visit she brought along with her a number of children's books, in particular, a Grade Three primer. Newspapers followed in quick succession. Clarence Brazier hadn't lost his touch. His past ability to adapt had now transcended to learning to read in what seemed to be record time. "I picked it up [reading] all by myself," laughed Clarence. "I read good (sic) by myself. I can read for hours. What I can't do is read to the public. Ask me to read out loud and I get stuck on the second word!"

Since moving to the outskirts of Sprucedale to live with his daughter, Doris, and son-in-law, retired OPP inspector Jim Villemaire, Clarence has been very involved in the Muskoka Literacy Council reading classes. His progress continues to "wow" everyone around him and his daughter is simply amazed at how much her father remembers from what he reads. One of his favourite stories is the children's version of the story of the *Titanic*. Said Doris, "My dad remembers this little obscure episode aboard ship concerning three dozen eggs. Now, how many people do you know would remember something like this when reading the history of the *Titanic*? My dad just seems to digest each word and remembers it." A few months after his 100th birthday, Canada Post presented Clarence Brazier with the National Literacy Award for 2006.

Despite his advanced age, Clarence continues to recite oral history to this day. And it's what had made him even keener to read about the past—his past. Some of his favourite reading material, says his daughter, is local history. "Maybe it's because I lived it," said Clarence with a twinkle in his eye.

A Century of Child Care in the Parry Sound District

The Parry Sound Children's Aid Society (CAS), now known as the Nipissing-Parry Sound CAS celebrates its centenary in 2009. Although in modern times its jurisdiction covers a vast region, it wasn't always so. In fact, during the first several decades of the 20th century, the Parry Sound CAS functioned as two entirely separate societies, one for the west side of the District and one for the east side. It is interesting to note that the Society's first inspector for East Parry Sound (Burk's Falls), John Hartill, earned more than three times the salary of his counterpart in the Town of Parry Sound. However, just how the local CAS functioned during the early years and why Hartill was paid the higher salary remains unclear, as the Society's archival records are spotty at best. Only a handful of annual reports remain from the East Parry Sound CAS, published by the Arrow Press in Burk's Falls—along with a few newspaper clippings from the *Burk's Falls Arrow* to supplement them.

Some of the issues of concern for the CAS in those very early days beginning in 1909, will raise a few eyebrows now. But they were seen as legitimate complaints, and investigations were launched on a regular basis. The complaints heard by the Society included delinquency, feeblemindedness, perceived insanity or drunkenness of the father, desertion, medical and moral neglect, the "violation of chastity," the illness or death of one parent, and finally, the imprisonment of a parent.

The greatest evil in the eye of the early CAS was an unemployed father. Surviving case records show that when fathers refused to work and support their families, they were sent to jail. For the CAS, the four most frequent causes of trouble inside the home included desertion, marital discord, non-support and finally, separation of the parents. To house the children in the Society's care there were just two CAS homes (or shelters as they were referred to in those days) for the entire district. The building housing the Burk's Falls Shelter is the only one to survive to this day and is now a private home located on the corner of Yonge and Main Street. The shelter for the Town of Parry Sound was originally located at 31 Miller Street.[1]

According to information provided in the CAS records, the earliest board meetings for the east side were held at the All Saints' Anglican Church Hall in Burk's Falls, with the CAS paying the church board $2 for the rental of the premises. The records also indicate that the occasional board meeting was held at the village's Hotel Central. Although it hasn't taken in lodgers for some years, the old hotel building located in the main business section of Burk's Falls still exists, its last occupant being a grocery store. From the smattering of old reports and newspaper clippings that have managed to survive, it can be surmised that at one point the matron at the Burk's Falls Shelter was Miss Minnie Dumble and the house physician was Dr. Milton A. Wittick. The two dentists who attended the children's dental needs were Drs. Kickham and Sloan. Mrs. Nettie (Knight) Hilliar is said to have donated "picture" papers on a weekly basis, while Mr. and Mrs. F. Wesley and James Wilson paid for the children's haircuts.

The man in charge of East Parry Sound's Children's Aid Society was John Hartill.[2] But who exactly was he? There are no records of Hartill having a family, although by following a trail of newspaper clippings from the *Burk's Falls Arrow*, it is known that he held the position of CAS inspector until at least the mid-1930s. This is approximately the time when the East and West Societies began holding joint annual meetings and by the late 1930s they had merged into one. The CAS's work then was divided into just three categories: investigations of the homes of non-wards where children were living at home under poor conditions; work with the wards directly under CAS care and legal adoptions; and investigations under the Unmarried Parents Act (UP). The latter cases were investigated with the prospects of getting the single mother married, or her child adopted.

What is known for certain about John Hartill is that he was a thirty-eight-year-old Englishman who had arrived in Canada alone sometime in 1911, spending his first few years in Toronto. While in the city he met John Kelso, the founder and first president of the Children's Aid Society. It was to become a lifelong friendship that charted a course for Hartill's own future with the CAS. By the time the two met, Kelso, who was a former newspaper reporter, had already firmly established himself as the champion of animals and small children. His book, *"The Early History of the Humane and Children's Aid Movement in Ontario"* was published the year Hartill came to Canada.

John Kelso was born in Dundalk, Ireland, on March 31, 1864, the youngest of nine Kelso children. The family immigrated to Toronto ten years later in October 1874. Immediately sent out to work to support the family, John did his best by doing errands and odd jobs for bits of food and a few pennies.[3] By the time he was twenty he was on the police beat for the Toronto *Globe* newspaper, and during the mid-1880s he witnessed first-hand the depraved conditions that many young children were forced to live in at the time. Although Kelso himself had for a time scrounged on the streets, the majority of the children he now saw were far worse off. As a night reporter he not only observed young newsboys sleeping in alleyways, he also watched them as they scampered off at daybreak to pick up the early edition. After his appeal to the Toronto Police to take a census, nearly 700 children were found to be living on the city's streets. And the census confirmed John Kelso's worst fears; these street urchins who spent their time begging or hawking small wares had no opportunity for a decent future.

Resolved to do something about it, he called for a meeting on February 24, 1887, to form the Toronto Humane Society. John Kelso was just 22. The purpose of this new Society at the close of the 19th century was to prevent cruelty to both animals and children. However, after just four years of operation Kelso realized that there was more public interest in protecting animals than children. So in 1891, John Kelso founded the Toronto Children's Aid Society, appointing himself as the first president. Two years later, in 1893, a law was finally passed in Ontario that protected children. Now aged twenty-nine, John Kelso became the first secretary, and later became the provincial Superintendent of Neglected and Dependent Children. The new law paved the way for a province-wide Children's Aid Society. Until his death in 1935, John Kelso worked tirelessly in the protection of both children and animals.[4]

It is likely that John Hartill was greatly influenced by his friend's social conscience, so much so that in 1915, after having decided to move out of the city, his own interest in child welfare was beginning to become a lifelong commitment. Hartill settled in Scotia Junction in Perry Township where census records indicate that he took up farming. He joined the Perry Township Agricultural Society in 1915, becoming its secretary treasurer on April 28, 1917[5] and held the position for one year. During the January 19, 1918, annual board meeting, members decided

By the time the Burk's Falls' Grand Trunk Railway station was completed in 1885, the second wave of settlers was making their way north. During its heyday, the train station located east of the village offered the most economical way to ship goods and passengers. Notice the Burk House "bus" service. This photo is believed to have been taken circa 1900. With the road system leaving much to be desired, the 1930s became the peak period for rail travel in the north. At the Burk's Falls' station, both passengers and freight were routinely dropped off and picked up. Unfortunately, it wasn't to last. Once moved away from the tracks, the former station would end its life as a machine shop for Boyes and Sons Construction Ltd. The station burnt to the ground in June 2000, a casualty of grinder sparks.

to appoint Charles White to the position of secretary treasurer and then offered him a salary of $80 a year to do the job, replacing Hartill. Up until this time it had been an unpaid position.[6]

During this time John Hartill was also the trustee and secretary-treasurer of the township's local school board. The school in Scotia (SS #2) was located on the William Hilliar farm, just west of the overhead bridge, south of the Scotia railway station. The first log schoolhouse had been replaced in 1888 with a more "modern" building when Perry Township was incorporated. By the time Hartill had settled in the community, a third schoolhouse had been built (c. 1910), with the old building serving as a woodshed until 1936.[7] It is now believed that his work with the school board is what led him to pursue his greater aspirations—child welfare. Once John Hartill was granted employment with the East Parry Sound CAS, he came to rely on his friendship with John Kelso. In fact, in 1919 Kelso loaned him an Underwood typewriter so that he could type out his reports. As inspector, John Hartill was the only paid person working in child welfare in East Parry Sound, earning an annual salary of $1,000. His counterpart in West Parry Sound earned just $300 a year.

For the first eleven years the East Parry Sound CAS concentrated its efforts in the larger towns—Scotia, Emsdale, Burk's Falls, Magnetawan, Sundridge and South River. It wasn't until 1920, and presumably under Hartill's direction, that any service was provided in the north end of the district, namely in the area of The Alsace, Arnstein, Golden Valley, Loring and Restoule. Shortly after the CAS began its work here, Society records make note of the Red Cross Outpost Hospital in Loring. It can be presumed that the mention of the hospital was in reference to the medical aid made available to local children in CAS care. However, before Henry Davis of Loring stepped forward to donate the land on which the hospital was eventually built, the community's first Red Cross nurse, Jean Haggart, elected to work from her home.[8]

Despite the fact that a trunk road was constructed to Port Loring in 1924[9] three years later, it became obvious to the residents that their community was still relatively isolated. North Bay was a great distance away. They needed their own hospital. That very same year a group of civic-minded residents arranged to rent the home of Mary and Joe Cain to house a makeshift medical facility.[10] A Miss Wiltshire is listed as the first nurse to work out of the Cain home, along with a Miss Austin. Wilma Weller was the housekeeper. In 1929, when the Red Cross Society obtained the land from Henry Davis, and the new hospital was built, all three ladies were offered positions which they accepted. Records show the Red Cross Outpost Hospital in Loring was spacious enough to accommodate five adults, along with three cribs for infants and one spare cot. Over time, six additional nurses were hired, including Misses Pearl Merriam, Reid (accompanied by a large police dog), Haywood, Livingston, McDiarmid and Rillett.[11]

By 1937, John Hartill had attained the position of superintendent of the CAS for the district. That same year, Parry Sound's Judge Moon, who presided over all CAS casework, commented that only 10 percent of the district's child welfare cases were in the Town of Parry Sound, with another 10 percent in the surrounding municipalities.[12] It is believed that West Parry Sound's modest caseload is what paved the way, in 1939, for the eventual merger of the two Societies. John Hartill retired from his post just five years later in 1943, at the age of seventy. By that time

During the Depression years when many rural people found themselves without work, boarding houses were the least expensive form of shelter. Careful scrutiny of the Armstrong Boarding House in Burk's Falls, photographed here in the mid-1930s, shows that the structure is, in fact, the east wing of the old Cataract House. The main part of the hotel burned down sometime during 1910. In later years the business was taken over by Percy and Josephine Brown and renamed Brown's Boarding House.

the Parry Sound Children's Aid Society records had noted a decrease in the number of children in the shelters. However, juvenile delinquency was on the rise. In both instances, CAS officials felt that the ongoing war in Europe might have had something to do with it.

Just a few years after Hartill's retirement, the Red Cross Outpost Hospital at Loring was identified as too small to serve the community's growing needs and efforts were made to find property on which to build a bigger facility. In 1949, a parcel of land situated between Loring and Port Loring was purchased from John Smith for $125. Smith became the caretaker of the new hospital while Misses Mona Zentler, Hilda Burch, Bailey and Tedders were hired on as nurses.[13] But as the years went by, local road conditions continued to improve, cutting down on the time it took to get to either of North Bay's two large hospitals. On September 30, 1970, Loring's little outpost hospital was ordered closed by the Red Cross Society. When the building was put up for tender, Helen Ristic, a registered nurse, bought the old hospital, turning it into a nursing home—White Eagle Home. However, by March 1978,

Ristic was in failing health. She closed the home and the patients were moved to the Lady Isabella Nursing Home in Trout Creek.[14]

Shelter Supporters

It is interesting to note that three of the Burk's Falls shelter's earliest supporters, Dr. Milton Wittick, Nettie Hilliar and James "Jim" Wilson, were so well known and thought of in the community that their names remain recognizable to this very day. In fact, in honour of the village doctor, the junior public school in Burk's Falls was eventually renamed in his memory. Dr. Wittick's life as a country doctor is best summed up in his autobiography, *The Doctor Who Never Refused a Call*, as told to Helen Maddeaux.[15]

As for Nettie Hilliar, she was the wife of the well-respected Burk's Falls businessman Joseph Frederick Hilliar. Because of her husband's successful business interests, Nettie had ample time on her hands to take on charitable work, including the CAS shelter. She was the daughter of Moses Knight of Bradford, Ontario, while Joseph was the son of British emigrants who had chosen Chicago as their first home. Joseph was born there in 1874. Four years after his birth, the Hilliar family decided to leave the United States for Canada, to take advantage of the province's offer of free land grants. Like the vast number of early settlers heading north, the Hilliar family took the train to Gravenhurst, then boarding a stagecoach to reach their destination, the hamlet of Scotia. It is here that Joseph's father, William Underhill Hilliar staked his claim.[16]

However, by 1880 the Hilliars were on the move again, this time to Frank Burk's little settlement on the banks of the Magnetawan River, where Joseph's father William, became the blacksmith. Being the fifth of eight Hilliar children, Joseph went to work at an early age to earn his keep. He started off as a clerk in Robert H. Menzies' General Store, and by 1899 felt secure enough financially to marry Mary Nettie Knight. The wedding took place on March 28, 1899, in her home town of Bradford. By the turn of the century, Joseph had gone into the hardware business with George Clark, a local resident. Joseph and Nettie lived above the store where their first son, Horace Knight, was born in December of 1900. Five years later Joseph bought the former Burk's Falls Arrow Press building on the corner of Yonge and Ontario streets, enlarging it to accommodate his ever-growing enterprise.

Joseph Hilliar had a good sense for business and always put his customers first, something that was widely known in the area. However, on a late winter's day in the year 1910, a newcomer to Burk's Falls was truly surprised by the "warm" reception by Hilliar. It was on St. Patrick's Day that the James Douglas family arrived at the Burk's Falls railway station, having come from Manitoba with a carload of cattle and furniture. Before going to breakfast at the Day House, one of the smaller hotels in existence at that time, James ordered a wood stove from the Hilliar Hardware Store to be delivered to their new farmhouse north of Burk's Falls. When the family arrived later that day, they discovered that Joseph Hilliar had not only delivered the stove but had also installed it—and had a fire going to warm the house.[17] Besides running the hardware

Dentist Dr. J.J. Wilson, left, and physician Dr. Milton Wittick were two early supporters of the Children's Aid Society (CAS) in Burk's Falls. Dr. Wilson arrived in the village at the turn of the 20th century to practise dentistry. For a number of years he was a director for the CAS while his wife was a missionary in China. He loved both children and animals and took great pride in his horse, Grace, that pulled his buggy around the village. When his wife died in the mid-1930s, Dr. Wilson took to tending to the local children under the care of the CAS and indulging in his passion for peonies and gladiolas.

business, Joseph Hilliar was also the clerk of the 4th Division Court, as well as the electrical bill collector for the Knight Bros. Eventually, he became the first Chevrolet dealer in Burk's Falls, combining furniture, cars and a funeral parlour on the list of his endeavours.

The third well-known early supporter of the CAS shelter was Jim Wilson. His father William had taken on the job of gaoler when the new courthouse was built in 1887, then became the village undertaker, and ultimately took an interest in the community's growing business section. He constructed a three-storey commercial block on the west side of the main street, where Jim and his family went to live after leaving the family homestead to his brother John. The ground floor was occupied by one of the village's two drugstores, while Jim and his family lived on the second floor. On the third floor the Masonic Lodge and concert hall shared equal space.[18] Unfortunately, on one cold winter's night, an explosion in the store portion of the building set the entire structure on fire. While Jim was attempting to save family possessions, he was hit in the head by falling brick. Rendered unconscious by the blow, Jim remained that way for several days and subsequently suffered ill health for several more weeks. The cause of the explosion was never determined, but by this time William Wilson was too old to rebuild.

Further misfortune was to strike the Wilson family. During a typhoid outbreak in the area, son John was stricken not once but three times. He was only forty when he finally succumbed to the dreaded disease. Employed by the Magnetawan Tannery Company, John had been busy with a shipment of tanbark at the railway station on a hot summer's day. To quench his thirst he drew water from a nearby well. He became sick, and it was later discovered that the well water was contaminated. John never recovered and four days later was dead, buried with three other men who also died of typhoid fever. John's wife Louise was left a widow at the age of twenty-eight, with four young children to raise and a farm to run. The tannery closed in 1922 after having being in operation for twenty-eight years.[19] Louise Wilson eventually sold the farm and moved into Burk's Falls with her children. She died at the relatively young age of fifty-eight.

It's been a long road to travel from the days when there were two societies, created simultaneously in October 1909. They eventually merged into one society in 1939 to be known as The Children's Aid Society of the District of Parry Sound. It would take another sixty years before the District's CAS evolved further to embrace the neighbouring District of Nipissing and rename itself The Children's Aid Society of the Districts of Nipissing and Parry Sound. For almost 100 years public support has remained steadfast. This support is still as necessary today and as relevant to the lives of the people of the area as it was nearly a century ago.

5
The South River Connection

Years before any permanent settler ventured this far north, the South River was primarily used by the lumber companies for floating logs to Lake Nipissing and points beyond. With its headwaters in Algonquin Park to the southeast of the present village, the South River meanders its way northwards, emptying into Lake Nipissing at South Bay. As far as the early lumbermen were concerned the considerable bends in its course made the river unsuitable for boat traffic, but despite its winding nature the South River was still a natural transportation corridor.[1]

The first actual government survey of the south shore of Lake Nipissing took place in 1858. For their headquarters, the surveyors chose South Bay, naming the area and the river "Namanitagong," which, roughly translated from Ojibwa, meant Red Chalk River. The mouth of the South River was ideally situated in a valley, surrounded on the west and southwest by hardwood hills. The river passed through the area from east to west, with the lake itself as the northern boundary. However, it would be four years after the survey was completed before the northern portion of the District of Parry Sound was opened up for settlement at a price of 50 cents an acre. The name Namanitagong was eventually changed to Nipissing Village and the challenge now for the prospective settler would be how to get there.[2]

The great colonization road stretching from the Village of Rosseau to Nipissing Village became the first link between established settlements in Muskoka and the northern wilderness. As prospective homesteaders continued to follow the construction of this road northward from Magnetawan, they began paying closer attention to the lands lying east towards the South River. To the untrained eye, these settlers reckoned that the land they viewed, once cleared of trees, was suitable for farming. Some of the first land claims in the area were registered just as the Rosseau-Nipissing Colonization Road was being hacked out through the forest. In fact, for many of these early settlers, to earn some much needed cash they joined the road crews in chopping down the trees to make way for the new road. Before 1900 just about all of the land lying east of the colonization road towards South River was registered under the Ontario Free Grants & Homestead Act. Many large acreages were cleared at once and put under cultivation. And when

By the turn of the 20th century, a number of settlers in Almaguin were finding their land claims unsuitable for cropping. Selling out to either the Standard Chemical Company or local lumbermen, the homesteaders joined the wave of settlers heading West. This postcard from 1908, depicting the Moosejaw District in Saskatchewan, shows both men and women proudly harvesting bumper crops of wheat.

these farms were new, bumper crops were harvested and large herds of cattle were kept. But, as was to happen in the district time and time again, the good soil was shallow and after a few years there was nothing left but sand, stones and rocks. A great majority of these farms were abandoned as settlers went in search of better land, leaving the forest to swallow up the buildings.[3]

One of the first lumber companies to acquire a timber licence in this area was the Fraser Lumber Company. In 1866, they set up the company's headquarters at the Big Bend on the South River, just west of the future town site of Powassan. John Fraser is credited for the initial improvements to the river system. The company began to build a series of dams and log slides to make it easier to float the logs over the South River's numerous rapids and waterfalls. Fraser had log slides built at the Chutes at Gimba, Cox, Davidson, Freeman and Gerber, along with the construction of a dam at Corkery Falls. Once all was completed, the lumberjacks set out to cut the pine forests along the river and float the logs down to Lake Nipissing. From there, the company's lumber and square timbers were loaded on scows and taken to North Bay. Once reloaded on to railway cars, the cargo was then shipped to southern ports where it was reloaded again, this time on to ships destined for England.

It was one thing to transport logs by water, but quite another to get the necessary supplies to the lumberjacks toiling deep in the forests. With no actual road system in place, provisions destined for the company's lumber camps in Laurier Township northeast of the South River, were hauled over blazed trails by teams hitched to homemade jumpers, sometimes for as far as forty kilometres.[4]

Following closely on the heels of the Fraser Lumber Company's lumberjacks, was John Rudolphus Booth of Ottawa. Considered the greatest lumber baron of the late 19th century, J. R. Booth had timber limits in and around Lake Nipissing, up the Sturgeon River and Duchesnay

Creek, as well as along the South River (Machar Township) and Trout Creek. In fact, any stream in the area that could float logs somehow wound up belonging to Booth. And on all of them he built dams and log slides to sluice his logs and square timber over the falls and rapids. The original dam at Trussler Bros. Mill in Trout Creek was built by Booth's employees. His men were also responsible for constructing the great log slides at the Chutes at Geisler, Chapman and Nipissing.

Booth harvested the pine from the Trout Creek and South River flats about 1889 and had them driven down to Lake Nipissing. The majority of the best quality trees were made into square timber, and, in separating the best from the rest, there were hundreds chopped down and left where they were felled.[5] Once at Lake Nipissing, Booth's logs were then boomed to Wasi Falls. Since the J.R. Booth Lumber Company's sawmills were in Ottawa, a plan was devised on how to get these logs to the mills. The solution was quite simple. Build a private railway from Lake Nosbonsing, which was part of the headwaters of the Ottawa River, to Lake Nipissing, near the mouth of the Wasi River. The logs could now be transferred from one lake to the other by rail. However, to complete each cycle of getting the logs out of the bush to the sawmills would take, for the most part, two logging seasons. During this time a fairly significant community sprang up at Wasi Falls, its inhabitants mostly the lumber company employees. However, just a few years after the Grand Trunk Railway was built through Callander to North Bay, J.R. Booth abandoned his railway. Although a few company houses were moved to Callander, much of Wasi Falls was left to fall into ruin.[6]

Once the homesteaders started pushing northwards to stake their claims in Machar and Laurier townships, smaller sawmills sprang up along the South River in direct competition to Booth's own mills. The first family to arrive by horse and wagon in 1881 and settle in the area was Robert Carter and his wife. The first sawmill was set up on the South River on Lot 1 Concession 2 by Charles Byrnes. He was soon joined by William Erb who also built his sawmill on the river, about a mile north in the southeast corner of Machar Township. The Erbs ran a general store in Kitchener, and in 1883 when William decided to try and make his fortune in the north, he loaded up a big furniture wagon with supplies, along with his wife and children, and set off. His eldest son remained behind to look after the family business. Occasionally, the son would send up a whole bolt of brightly coloured gingham to his parents, and Mrs. Erb would make clothes for the entire family including shirts for William, all out of this same cloth.[7]

Sometime later, a Mr. McAdams would build a shingle mill close to Byrnes, while Mr. Shannon's sawmill was at The Narrows on Eagle Lake, also in Machar Township. These small mills were cutting lumber and shingles for the settlers who needed the materials for the roofs and floors of their log shanties and stables. At first things were fairly amiable between the homesteaders and lumber companies. When the log drives came down the South River each summer, the cooks on these drives bartered flour, salt pork, beans, molasses and tea to the settlers in exchange for eggs, milk, butter, buttermilk and vegetables. The homesteaders welcomed the additional food staples and the farm produce was a welcome change to the river drivers who tired from the monotonous daily fare of bread, beans, black-strap molasses and sowbelly.

At the time the provincial government was standing firm on its policy that all the pine trees on the land claims were to be included in the timber licences held by the lumber companies, except for that the homesteader figured he needed to build his own cabin and shelter for his livestock. It soon became apparent that when it came to the timber rights, the lumber companies meant business, leaving the smaller mill operators out in the cold. One unlucky homesteader would learn the lesson the hard way. James Jones had situated his homestead on the shores of Eagle Lake and went about the task of cutting and skidding about 500 pine logs on his claim. Jones intended to take the logs to Shannon's and have them milled into lumber. His plan was to use some of the lumber as building material and the rest as payment to the mill. J.R. Booth, who held the timber licence, had other ideas. Before James Jones could get the logs to Shannon's, all but sixty of them were seized by a gang of Booth's men and dumped into the South River with the rest of the company's haul. Jones didn't receive one cent for the logs.[8]

However, when the teamsters tried the same tactic on another area homesteader, the outcome was quite different. William Smyth had also been cutting down a considerable quantity of pine, but when Booth's men arrived with their sleighs to claim "their share" of the logs, Smyth was waiting for them. Sitting on the skidway with a loaded shotgun across his knees, he was not about to budge. The teamsters weren't about to mess with him and simply left. With Smyth's claim so far back in the bush and with the end of the cutting season rapidly approaching and the snow about to melt, the lumber company wouldn't bother going after this homesteader's logs. There would be more than enough logs to contend with in the river, all needing to be boomed to Lake Nipissing. As for Booth getting the authorities out to deal with the rogue homesteader, it simply wasn't worth his time. In the end, William Smyth got his logs to Shannon's mill.[9]

By the turn of the 20th century, more and more settlers began arriving in Machar and Laurier townships. In fact, scores of people came to South River via the Grand Trunk Railway, all eager to settled down and build homes. The original South River Lumber Company had been established to ensure a steady supply of building materials. Soon there were many more businesses being set up in the small community. These included: the South River Mercantile Company, Robert M. Carter Shoe Store, Vincent Company Store, West End Supply Depot, Messrs. Shaw and Ryan, A.E. Ballard Meat Store, W.A. Connelly Planing Mill, watchmaker W.H. Chapman and Jard Wait, who sold carriages and was engaged in woodworking repairs. It wasn't long after this that the South River Lumber Company started operations in Laurier Township and turned to shipping lumber on the railway. When the Turner Bros. Lumber Company of North Bay started logging in Paxton Township in 1901, the South River Lumber Company, with its large sawmill on the river, was contracted to transform Turner's logs into lumber. Besides sawing their own logs, that first summer the mill cut 10,000,000 board feet for the Turner Bros. as well. But, as it would turn out, the contract with Turner Bros. would not last long. The North Bay company was only interested in extracting the best of the pine timber in Paxton Township, and within six years they had cleared out what they wanted and abandoned the licence.

Despite this setback, the mill in South River did expand and was modernized to cut 125,000 board feet per day. The saws operated day and night, with a steam-driven dynamo (generator) installed to light up the mill and mill yard. But by 1908, the year after South River separated from Machar Township to officially become a village, hydroelectric power was being generated. Now, the lumber company's trolleys used to haul the lumber from the mill to the yard were electrically operated. A second expansion included a lath mill where 50,000 wooden laths per day were cut out of the pine slabs left over from the sawmill. To pay its employees, the South River Lumber Company didn't have a payroll as such, but used "scrip," a certificate which the men could use at the company store for groceries, tobacco and clothing.[10] W.J. Ard was the village's first reeve; he co-owned the South River Mercantile Company.

There is no doubt that the original South River Lumber Company helped boost the growth of the community. However, it would be the Standard Chemical Company that would bring a new kind of wealth to this northern settlement.

The Standard Chemical Company

When, in 1904, the Standard Chemical Company, with its head office in Montreal, decided to establish a factory in South River to manufacture wood alcohol, residents couldn't believe their luck. The company had developed a new process to extract alcohol and a number of other chemicals such as acetic acid and acetone from wood (the latter chemical being used to make explosives). The region had been left littered with scrap hardwood by the lumbermen and the settlement of South River was situated smack in the middle of the debris. It wasn't long after the chemical company opened its doors before the Sovereign Bank established itself in South River to look after the banking needs of both the community and its growing businesses.[11]

Up until the First World War, chemicals were the chief product of Standard Chemical Company, and its list of factories would expand to include parts of England and Europe. Closer to home, homesteaders in Laurier Township who were sick and tired of years of unsuccessful cropping, were only too glad to accept what the chemical company offered for their claims. Loading up their belongings, they joined the wave of settlers migrating to western Canada. Their departure would leave only a few farms in the area, mostly on the first concession where soil conditions were better. The majority of these were farmed until the 1960s.[12]

Owning the timber licence on the Crown lands in Laurier Township along with the numerous land claims they acquired, the Standard Chemical Company's plant in South River became one of the more successful operations of the six built in Ontario in the early 1900s. Ideally situated, the plant made good use of its wood resources to meet the demand for wood alcohol and charcoal. They used the good trees for sawlogs and made cordwood out of the poorer quality hardwood trees. The cordwood went to the chemical plant where charcoal, wood alcohol and acetate of lime were manufactured. It wasn't too many years before the Village of South River became known as "Charcoal Town." The Standard Chemical Company became the largest employer in South River, and to ensure a steady supply of wood, the company bought the Turner Bros. abandoned timber licence in Paxton Township.

The Standard Chemical Company in South River was one of six plants built in Ontario during the early 1900s. This photograph, taken from a postcard, depicts the water tank and factory office. Over the years the office staff would include Ross Chemmens as plant manager, Howard Mitchell, Wilfred Johnston, Bert Anderson, and Jeff Lydiatt, along with secretaries Elsie McIssac and Miss McGibbon.

After the war, with the price of Pennsylvania coal (the source of their fuel) skyrocketing, the chemical plant was shut down temporarily. However, when, shortly after this closure, the Longford Mills near Orillia exhausted its supply of available timber, Standard Chemical Company officials began the search for a new source of timber. The forest east of South River still had some good stands of birch and maple, and in the 1920s there was a renewed demand for hardwood. The decision was to move the Longford mill here. Bob Robertson, a millwright, assisted in setting up the new sawmill. South River was now home to two sawmills as there were still plenty of trees to go around.[13]

Frank Cooper, the woods manager for the Standard Chemical Company recognized that although the plant had ceased operations, there was still a wealth of hardwood in the bush. He wanted his son Orlo (also spelled Orly) to tap into this hardwood, not only in Laurier, but Ballantyne Township as well. In 1924, he persuaded Orlo to leave the Laidlaw Lumber Company of Toronto and come to South River to take over the day to day running of the milling operations of Standard Chemical, under his direction.

In the early days in order to haul logs out of the bush a trestlework bridge of about 305 metres had been constructed across the South River. In 1917, a standard gauge railway, built by a local contractor, Barney Wickett, was laid over this bridge and continued for ten kilometres towards Algonquin Park. The track needed to be extended in order to tap into the best cordwood

This photograph of a postcard shows the wood yard of the Standard Chemical Company in South River. The company's rail line provided easy access into the bush where cut sawlogs could be loaded and transported back to the mill. In 1946, the steel rails were lifted and replaced by a truck road.

timber limits, the road conditions being too abysmal to permit any other access. In the 1920s, trucks simply weren't capable of doing the work. Orlo Cooper was quoted at the time as saying, "When I came up here, you couldn't haul anything by truck. They were wrecking axles all the time if you put heavy loads on them." Orlo has been credited as the one responsible for having the bridge rebuilt and adding approximately forty kilometres to the existing railway, extending it right to Round Lake. However, before the railway extension could be completed, the first logging camps were already being set up the winter of 1924–25. By January the camps were in high gear and making use of "ice roads." These roads went over frozen lakes to make transportation of the logs to the mill that much easier.[14]

When the chemical company's sawmill began operating in the summer of 1925, it had a unique piece of equipment termed a "hog." This hog was capable of grinding up the slab wood and edgings, which were then shipped south to the Huntsville tannery to be used as fuel. About twenty to thirty cords of hog fuel were produced daily, and, according to Orlo Cooper, the mill was shipping somewhere around three gondola cars a day to the tannery. "My father saw this, and figured the chemical plant could use that fuel too, instead of expensive imported coal." As a result, A.F. Cooper reopened the Standard Chemical Plant in 1926, and it was to remain open until the late 1950s.

For a time its chief product would remain wood alcohol, which was recovered at about nine gallons per cubic cord of wood. The South River operation was comprised of a twelve-oven wood distillation plant with each oven capable of handling six cords of hardwood (mainly maple) on a daily basis, or approximately 26,000 cords of wood annually.[15] Arvi Vanello is listed as being in charge of the hardwood. From 1926 to 1951, the chemical plant had a workforce that averaged about 100 employees, while the sawmill, planing mill and railway employed an additional 105 men. Over the years, the office staff at the chemical plant in South River included Ross Chemmens as plant manager, and Howard Mitchell, Wilfred Johnston, Bert Anderson and Jeff Lydiatt, along with secretaries, Elsie McIssac and Miss McGibbon.[16]

Although the plant was primarily using the hog fuel in its operations, there were many men being employed as cordwood cutters. According to Art Loney, lead teamster in the Standard Chemical yard, when a lumber camp area had been "cut over," the foreman and his men moved to another area camp. The cordwood cutters then would move into the vacated camp to clean up. Art's father Bill was also a teamster for the company "right up until they shut down." A.F. Cooper is said to have brought Italians and Finlanders into the country to supplement the workforce in the bush. The bush foremen at Camp 4 were: first Bill Holt, followed by George Furlong, then Art Wood and Walter Frost. When Wood became ill, Jim MacIntosh filled in as the foreman for one year. At one point, Art Wood was also a sawyer for the company. Others listed as sawyers include Jack Berton, Jim Nicklon and Bob Everest.

One of the most important things about working in the camps was the food. If the food was good, it kept the men there. One lumberjack by the name of Adams remembers carrying a fifty-pound butter box into the bush full of food for lunch. The menu consisted of salt pork, cheese, homemade bread and corn syrup. "We took turns carrying lunch for twelve to fourteen men, it was no fun," recalls Adams.[17] Of course, there also were cooks, such as George James, Norm Ullman, Dave McLish, Tommy Bush, Martin Iverson and Earl Conn, hired to work right in the camps.[18] According to Art Loney, "You didn't walk right in and sit down before combing your hair. We were nice and clean before sitting down to the meal."

With the onset of the Depression, there would be many unemployed men in this rural community desperate to feed their hungry families. The Standard Chemical Company in South River was seen as coming to their rescue. The company's cordwood and logging camps ballooned in size, employing anywhere from 150 to 350 men at a time. Art Loney recalls many desperate farmers coming down from Trout Creek with their teams of horses to work for Standard Chemical. Two logging camps were in operation every winter, remembered Orlo Cooper, with even the company sawmill kept going, thus providing men work for $1 day. "We paid them more of course, when times got better," added Cooper. "That first camp we had when times were really tough, well, the men were so good I got as much wood out there as if I had two camps going." The company went out of its way to assist its workforce. "Sometimes we didn't get any more than $26 a month," said Art Loney, "but it was enough to keep us going. There was no place else to go." In the late 1930s and early 1940s, Standard Chemical Company owned twenty-six houses in the village's east end that it rented out to its employees. Rents ranged from $3.75 to $10 a month. A few of those homes have survived to this day.[19]

From 1926 to 1951 the Standard Chemical Company had a workforce that averaged about 100 employees, while the sawmill, planing mill and railway employed an additional 105 men. This group photograph, taken at the side of one of the company sheds, is believed to date from between 1926 and 1928. The workers are from the chemical division.

Fortunately for the Standard Chemical Company, although there were millions of board feet of lumber being stockpiled during the Depression because the labour was so cheap, once the market recovered the company was able to unload it all at a profit. However, by the time the Second World War broke out and men started to enlist, the workforce all but dried up. Orlo Cooper had to find another solution—and he did.

There were about 100 German POWs being held at Pettawawa at the time, and Cooper was able to convince military authorities to put about forty prisoners, ones that spoke English, to work at the Standard Chemical Plant's logging camps near South River. The majority of the Germans worked at Camp 10, which was located in the middle of Paxton Township and accessed by the company railway. Unarmed guards were on duty while the prisoners worked with the Park Ranger Dan Stringer who was never far away.

Stringer was headquartered at Camp 10 where the POWs were sequestered. According to Art Loney, "Old Dan didn't mind and was right in there with them [the POWS]. Never missed a meal at the camp. He got along with everybody."

Pictured here in a close-up of the group photograph of Standard Chemical Company's employees are Arthur Reeds (left) and Peter Murdock, both plant managers.

Dan "Mud" Stringer at the age of fifty, posing with a lake trout taken from North Tea Lake. According to his daughter Gail Maeck, a lake trout of this size was a typical catch for the time. Dan was raised in Algonquin Park and was a park ranger there for forty years.

Dan Stringer was a park ranger for forty years, retiring in 1960. When he passed away on December 15, 1975, Hartley Trussler, a local journalist subsequently penned a newspaper column on Dan and Camp 10. The Trusslers were not strangers to the area. Hartley's father, James Trussler, had homesteaded in Trout Creek, just north of South River, and Hartley knew Dan Stringer personally, It was during the war years that Hartley gained valuable insights on the goings-on at the POW camp. He was holding down a government job inspecting food rationing, when one day a German POW lodged a complaint. Hartley headed for South River to see Dan Stringer. The visit became the basis of that 1975 column. "I was a little concerned about going into Camp 10 but needn't have been because Dan Stringer had become quite friendly with most of them [POWs] and introduced me and acted as an intermediary. We had our supper with them and it was as good a meal as you could wish for. After supper we had a meeting during which they told me their troubles and we had a very friendly discussion. By the way, they were given exactly the same rations as the local people. They were quite a fine gang of men, clean, well-groomed and well-behaved." Art Loney's perspective was equally positive, "Those prisoners were the best thing that ever happened to us. Standard Chemical workers benefited from everything they got. We used to have our drinking water in a pail and got it out with a dipper. When the prisoners arrived, well, we got paper cups."[20] The police stationed in Burk's Falls were called out on several occasions when prisoners tried to escape, but the "escapes" have never been substantiated. It is known that on occasion the German prisoners would go on "walks" and get lost for upwards of three days before stumbling back into the camp, scratched and mosquito bitten.[21]

By the end of the war, road conditions were finally being improved and trucks were being used more and more. "Originally, our railway ran very close to the logging camps," recalled Orlo Cooper. "We would use teams of horses and sleighs to pull the logs out of the bush and then load them onto the rail cars." Cooper was to remain in South River until his father retired in 1945. Shortly afterwards he was relocated to Standard Chemical Company's head office in Toronto where he took over as woods manager. Ross Chemmens became the manager at the South River plant and after him, Bert Anderson. However, Cooper wouldn't completely sever his ties with the community where had he'd spent over twenty years. His schedule would see him just one day a week at the Toronto office, with two days spent at Harcourt in the Haliburton area and two days in South River. Ted Brooks, the son of Les Brooks who was a long-time employee of Standard Chemical in South River, was appointed the woods manager at Harcourt. When truck transportation became more cost efficient, the Standard Chemical Company lifted the steel rails in 1946 and converted the rail bed into a truck road.[22]

In the beginning, wood alcohol had been the chief product of the Standard Chemical Company with charcoal strictly a sideline. But over the years its production would increase many times over. In May of 1946, something unexpected happened. A fire broke out and burned down a storage shed and two buildings where the charcoal processing took place. It was impossible to put out the flames quickly as all the structures were of wooden frame construction, sheathed in corrugated iron sheeting. Following the fire, there was some debate by officials at the chemical company's head office as to whether they should bother with the reconstruction. Times were

At one time, the Standard Chemical Company in South River was the largest employer in the area. Pictured here is a full complement of workers, including two women from the office (standing inside shed door opening) and several of the employees' children. Village historians would write, "The Standard Chemical Company will always be remembered by the people of South River. It gave the town the economic boost that was badly needed when times were difficult."

changing, and along with new technology and a softening of the market, there were fears that Standard Chemical Company's days were numbered. But ultimately the decision was to go ahead and rebuild at the South River location.

While the reconstruction was taking place, Len Baxter was already Standard Chemical's superintendent of factories, with A.J. Murdoch holding down the position of superintendent of the South River plant. For Baxter, his entire working life in Canada would be spent as an employee of the Standard Chemical Company. Arriving in Canada in 1905 from Yorkshire, England, he obtained his first position as an office boy in Montreal. In 1910, he was relocated to Longford Mills outside of Orillia. But from 1910 to 1931, the chemical company would move Baxter between Montreal and Orillia a number of times before offering him a permanent position in South River. Len Baxter remained there until his retirement in 1955. Over his many years with the company, Baxter would work with such individuals as W. G. Provencal, oven foreman, Ernie Lamb, oven-pulling foreman, and office manager G. F. (Rusty) Hanson. A few years before his retirement, Baxter would work with Albert McConaghy, the woods and plant manager, along with Gordon Watte, the master mechanic.[23]

The year 1946 was a turning point for the Standard Chemical Company as profits started dwindling from its Ontario and Quebec plants. K.S. McLaughton of Toronto was the company president and Edward Plunket Taylor the chairman of the board. It would be during E.P. Taylor's tenure as chairman that the restructuring process became most pronounced. Although locally, there were those who felt things should remain as they were, officials at the head office believed that if the chemical company expected to survive much longer, changes were necessary. For one thing, Taylor felt that forestry engineers were now needed to improve overall production. Two of the engineers who would spend some time at South River were Bill Hooper and a B. Bartlett.

As it would turn out, E. P. Taylor's keen eye for business would lead him to become one of Canada's most aggressive industrialists. It would be right after the Second World War, during the time he was the chairman of Standard Chemical, that he founded his own investment company, the Argus Corporation. Becoming its major shareholder, E.P. Taylor gained control of a number of Canadian companies including Dominion Tar and Chemical of Montreal that, in 1951, bought out the Standard Chemical Company. Taylor then sold the chemical company's timber rights, including those in Parry Sound District, to Hay & Company of Woodstock.[24]

In 1955, the year Len Baxter retired, the chemical company would change hands again, this time being acquired by Ray Industries Incorporated of Oxford, Michigan. Then, just four years later, the company was sold again. By 1959 the new owners were another American Company, the Arcan Company.[25] Interestingly enough, despite E.P. Taylor's business successes, many of the companies he had dealings with like Standard Chemical Company, no longer exist in the 21st century. What does survive however is the E.P. Taylor name and that of his beloved racehorse—the country's greatest thoroughbred—*Northern Dancer*.

From 1959 onwards, despite a number of initiatives to make the Standard Chemical Company property in South River a going concern, nothing seemed to take hold. Ultimately, the company was shut down and the buildings dismantled. Its lands adjacent to the South River at the east end of town were allowed to grow into a tangle of grass, weed and brush. It is hard to imagine that some eighty-five years ago this was once the site of a prosperous chemical plant and lumber mill. Harder still, is to picture the causeway over the South River as the company's private railway. Eastward along Chemical Road, over the river and into Algonquin Park, this was the route that for twenty-five years Standard Chemical Company used to transport hardwood timber to its mill.[26]

Fortunately, just in time for the celebration of the village's centenary in 2007, the municipality has done much to reclaim the former chemical company lands by grooming it into a public park—named Tom Thomson Park. The revitalization has brought a "greening" process to South River. Restoration is also underway of the historic 1885 Grand Trunk Railway station located just minutes away from this public park. All that is left from the company's glory days is the name, Chemical Road. A few years back there was a strong push to have the street renamed, but in the end history won out. Correspondence contained in the archives of the South River-Machar Union Public Library, aptly put it the company's historic significance in to just two sentences: "The Standard Chemical Company will always be remembered by the people of South River. It gave the town the economic boost that was badly needed when times were difficult." Art Loney couldn't agree more.

Arthur G. Peuchen: A Survivor

Just who was behind the fortunes of the Standard Chemical Company? It turns out it was a military man from Toronto by the name of Arthur Godfrey Peuchen. According to a number of historical records not only is Peuchen recognized as one of the first individuals in the world to manufacture acetone from wood, he also actually perfected the plans for extracting chemicals from waste hardwoods—chemicals such as acetone, acetic acid, acetate of lime, methanol and formaldehyde. Although he would receive many accolades for his discovery and was the president of the Standard Chemical Company from 1897 to 1914, Arthur Peuchen would never recover from being branded a coward. What was his dastardly deed? Major Arthur Peuchen survived the sinking of the *Titanic* in 1912. After the disaster, rumours about the major were rampant. His later attempts to discredit the *Titanic*'s Captain Edward J. Smith in the New York newspapers only aggravated Peuchen's situation. It also didn't help that Peuchen shared Lifeboat 6 with the "unsinkable" Molly Brown.[1] Apparently Peuchen complained of tiredness and balked at the idea of taking his turn to row, until goaded by Mrs. Brown. Or so the story goes.

Born in Montreal on April 18, 1859, Arthur was the son of Godfrey Peuchen of Westphalia, Prussia, and Eliza Eleanor Clark of Hull, England. Arthur's father had been a railway contractor in South America while his grandfather had managed the London, Brighton and Midlands Railway in England. After attending private schools in Montreal, in 1871, Arthur would move to Toronto where he eventually enlisted in the Queen's Own Rifles. He would rise through the ranks becoming a lieutenant in 1888, a captain in 1894 and a major in 1904. In 1893 he married Margaret Thompson, the daughter of John Thompson of Orillia. Peuchen's ultimate glory was serving as the marshalling officer at the coronation of George V on June 22, 1911.

However, it was his passion for sailing that many have pointed to as his possible undoing. He owned his own yacht, the *Vreda*, and during the period of time that Canadian playboy John Hugo Ross[2] lived in Toronto, Peuchen was part of his crew. So taken by sailing, and with his Standard Chemical Company having offices not only in Ontario and Quebec, but England, France and Germany as well, Arthur Peuchen looked forward to his numerous trips abroad. When he boarded the *Titanic* at Southampton on April 10, 1912, it would be his 40th transatlantic voyage. At the time, first-class tickets cost £30. 10s. Although the ship's manifest lists that that both Peuchen and Ross travelled first-class (both the major's ticket, number #113785, and that of Ross, number #13049, are included in the *Titanic* documentation), Ross is said to have been so ill with dysentery that he was carried by stretcher to his cabin. There is some speculation that Arthur Peuchen may have been the last person to see John Hugo Ross alive, as presumably, he drowned in his bed when the *Titanic* sank.

What has been fairly well-documented is Peuchen movements shortly after the *Titanic* began sinking. Already on deck, the major took keen notice of Lifeboat 6 as it was being lowered over the side. The ship's quartermaster, Robert Hichens (also spelled Hitchens), was sitting in the lifeboat and shouting for help. Peuchen apparently turned to the *Titanic*'s Second Officer Charles Herbert Lightoller and informed him he was willing to offer his assistance as he was a yachtsman. Given the official go-ahead by the ship's captain, Edward J. Smith, Peuchen is said to have scrambled into Lifeboat 6 during its descent into the water. Later, the conduct of both Hichens and the major would come under close scrutiny during official inquiries into the sinking. There was much conflicting testimony and those that wondered out loud how a military man would tolerate Hichens' apparent cowardly conduct in such a time of crisis.[3] However, there were others who felt that Peuchen, the military man, would never have second-guessed an officer in charge least it be viewed as mutiny.

Despite the public condemnation, Peuchen was to receive his promotion to lieutenant-colonel in the Queen's Own Rifles on

Courtesy of Mrs. Frank Rowntree, property of Burk's Falls and District Museum

When the First World War began, many of the local youth rushed to enlist. The recruiting office in Burk's Falls was located at the north end of the Sharpe Block. This photograph of Privates Edward Cook and Dave Cawthra (in front), with Dave's brother, George Cawthra, standing in the back, was taken overseas.

May 21, 1912. When the First World War broke out, he resigned his position as president of Standard Chemical Company to take command of the Home Battalion of his regiment. However, after the war was over Arthur Peuchen began his downward spiral. In the 1920s, a string of bad investments caused him to lose most of his money. The fact he had survived not only the sinking of the *Titanic* but World War I as well and then his wealth seemingly proved to be just too overwhelming. Records tell us that Peuchen wound up destitute and alone, but there are conflicting reports on how and where he died. Some believe his last four years were spent in a boarding house in Hinton, Alberta, where he died of pneumonia in 1929. There are other reports that he managed to return to Toronto that summer, only to die at his home at #104 Roxborough Street East on December 7. He is buried in Mount Pleasant Cemetery, along with his wife Margaret who died in 1951.

As for Hichens, following his testimony at the *Titanic* inquiries, which were held on both sides of the Atlantic, he continued on as a seaman. In the late 1920s, he and his wife, Florence Mortimore, and their children, Florence, Freddie, Edna, Doreen and Robert moved to the English harbour town of Torquay, Devon. However, by 1931 his family had left him and had gone back to Southampton. At this point Robert Hichens is said to have turned to the bottle. In 1933, he was arrested for the attempted murder of Harry Henley and spent the next four years in jail. Released in 1937, Hichens is said to have died onboard the cargo ship *English Trader*, on September 23, 1940, and was buried at sea.[4]

In the early years at least, Arthur Peuchen held a controlling interest in the Standard Chemical Company, with South River as one of the six locations chosen as a factory site in Ontario. Although his life appeared far removed from the everyday grind of the company workers, in the end, Peuchen and his employees were to suffer the same fate. There was nothing left when the factory doors closed for the last time.

Pickerel River Logging Days

By the 1870s the supplies of standing pine in eastern Ontario had all but disappeared, but not the demand. The American West was hungry for building material and a new source was desperately needed to fill the void. As the lumbermen's eyes turned to the north shore of Lake Huron, it was gold they imagined flowing into Georgian Bay down the vast rivers of the French and its tributaries, the Pickerel and Wanapitei. The lumbermen understood all too well that these rivers were natural transportation corridors that could be easily used for moving logs culled from the region's leftover timber stands. In 1872, when a government official by the name of Thomas Foster opened up the limits on the remaining Crown lands around the French River, the rush was on.[1] One of the first companies to set up was Walkerton Lumber. With the waters of the Pickerel River streaming off the French River and running smoothly inland for several miles, during the first few seasons at least, the company inched its way from its outlet on the French River, proceeding further and further upstream to clear-cut its quota of logs. From its headquarters at the mouth of the river, these logs were then boomed to the company's mills further south along the Georgian Bay coastline.

However, it wasn't long before a consortium of lumbermen not only bought out Walkerton Lumber Company, but also the timber rights to hundreds of miles of pine, thus forming the American Lumber Company—later to be renamed the Ontario Lumber Company (OLC).[2] The lumber conglomerate was headed by Herman H. Cook and included his wife Lydia, Frank E. MacDonald, John Melville Dollar and Frederick Hannell.[3] Having constructed a huge sawmill at the mouth of the French River, the OLC milled its sawlogs there before loading the lumber onto barges destined for the big cities on the lower Great Lakes. From those city ports, some of the lumber would be shipped to Montreal then reloaded onto ocean-going vessels heading for England.

However, the OLC's first task was to first get its men and supplies into the lumber camps before any logging could take place. Everything the company needed was transported by big paddlewheel steamboats that routinely plied the waters of Georgian Bay. The steamers made regular stops at the wharf located near the sawmill and the men travelled inland from there on smaller boats or pointers. The pointer boats were so called because of their long, sharp-pointed ends, which allowed the men to reverse direction without having to actually turn the boat around. As a rounded V-bottomed rowboat, each vessel, depending on its length, was outfitted with a minimum of six, 25-pound oars.[4] If the river was full of logs the oars would be rendered useless, but the river drivers would simply resort to poling their way through the logs with pike poles. In this fashion, the boats could be easily manoeuvered up the Pickerel River to Kidd's Landing on Squaw Lake in Mowat Township, which was the end of water navigation.[5]

In order for the loggers to reach the various camps situated within the company's timber limits, they would walk along tote roads that had been blazed through the woods. These early "roads" were nothing more than narrow tracks that snaked around stumps and rocks, with corduroy (the crosslays of logs) built across marshes and low spots. Two of the most well-known tote roads included the one from Byng Inlet, which ran south of the Magnetawan River to as far east as Deer Lake in McKenzie Township, and the road running from the north side of the Still River, east to Kelcey Lake in Wilson Township. Tote roads were also the lifeline of the depot camps. It was at these camps that additional supplies were warehoused and where company horses were pastured for the summer months. One of the biggest depot camps in the area belonged to the Ontario Lumber Company, located on lot 13, concession 9, in McConkey Township, about fifteen miles north of Loring. Other lumber companies that started up around

The Holland-Graves Lumber Company (later Graves and Bigwood) built a large, modern (by 1900s standards) sawmill on the eastern end of navigation on the Magnetawan River, close to where the Still River enters Georgian Bay at Byng Inlet. This early postcard shows the mill during the heyday of logging, its yard and pond full of logs.

the same time as the OLC but never quite reached the same magnitude, included the Victoria Harbour Lumber Company with its timber licence to cut white pine logs on lots surrounding Dollars Lake,[6] Turner Bros. of North Bay with its limits in Wilson and Paxton townships, Hardy Lumber in Hardy Township, McCormick and Irwin and finally Holland-Graves (later Graves and Bigwood) with its big sawmill situated at Byng Inlet. The latter company also had logging rights around the Magnetawan River.[7]

Although all these early lumber companies, both big and small, utilized a system of tote roads, after freeze-up each one of them was in the same situation. The harsh reality of winter setting in completely severed ties to the outside world. Lumberjacks who would head for the camps in September or October wouldn't get out until sometime after the first of May. For those who could read and write, not only was there no way to get a letter home—there was no way to get any mail in. It was a dilemma faced by the lumber company officials as well, as winter meant there would be no communication with head offices in Toronto.[8]

One company to come up with a solution to this ongoing problem was the Ontario Lumber Company. In 1882, it built a winter road connecting its logging camps in Parry Sound, Rosseau and Bracebridge to the railhead at Gravenhurst. Known as the Pickerel Hills Road, it ran southward from the OLC's depot camp in McConkey Township through Loring and past Arnstein, where it angled in a southeasterly direction before crossing the Pickerel River at Lot 23 Concession 2 in Mills Township. Eventually, it connected with the Rosseau-Nipissing Colonization Road at Glenila and the Great North Road, joining the latter at a point about ten miles north of Dunchurch.[9]

One of the earliest "mailmen" to travel the OLC's winter road between the company's five north-end lumber camps was Albert McCallum. His responsibility was to deliver mail along an eighty-kilometre route. He was known as "Mac" by the local settlers and it is said that the homesteaders along the road would wait for him to pass and then look at their clocks to see if their timepieces were running accurately—ironic, considering the man didn't own a watch and had no time schedule to follow. On the Monday morning, he'd leave the depot camp in McConkey Township, carrying the mailbag on his back. His first stop would be Glenila where he would get something to eat before heading to Dunchurch. Here, Mac picked up any in-coming mail as well as supplies. Carrying an average of fifty pounds a load, he would then return to Glenila to spend the night, leaving the next morning to arrive back at the depot camp by noon. Mac habitually made the 160-kilometre round trip on foot in a day-and-a-half, making his way along the unploughed road with only the occasional sleigh track or two to make the journey easier.[10]

In the early days the majority of lumber camps did not keep ready cash on the premises to pay the workers. The preferred option was to send the company clerk once a month to Parry Sound to pick up the payroll. In the case of the Ontario Lumber Company, one such trip would have dire consequences. One fall day back in the 1880s, as the company clerk was heading back to camp, he had a change of heart. For whatever reason, he decided to steal the money, hide it and come back for it later. It was almost dark and still some distance from the depot camp when the clerk stopped the horses and removed the money from the wagon. Unfortunately for him, just as he was hiding the stash the team took off. Whatever had spooked the horses caused them to pound along the tote road at a frightening pace. As the team raced towards the camp, sections of the wagon were flying off, as were the camp supplies. The thunderous noise of the horses' hooves as they crossed the Blaney Creek Bridge alerted the teamsters back at the camp to the fact that something was terribly wrong. When the team finally arrived, they were dragging the wagon's front wheels behind them—that's all that was left. Everyone at the depot camp headed down the tote road, only to find pieces of the wagon, its freight and the mail, strewn all along the way for a considerable distance. However, what was missing was the payroll. The clerk joined in the futile search in hopes of directing the men away from where he had hidden the money. Although there was some debate on what had happened to the payroll, the matter was soon dropped—that is until a week later.

As the teamsters headed off to the stables one night after supper to tend to their horses, they heard the sound of an approaching wagon. It was the same thunderous noise as the first time around. But it never got any closer, and finally disappeared. Two years later the clerk finally got up enough nerve to venture back to retrieve the payroll. He was in for a shock. In those two years the area had been cut over, changing the terrain so dramatically that he couldn't find the money. He left, his hopes dashed. It would be more than seventy years before anyone would hear the "wild wagon" again.

When August and Ida Parolin were married in 1916, the site of old OLC depot camp was their wedding present from their friend, John Fraser of the Fraser Lumber Company. One day years later, in 1958, when Ida Parolin was alone at the camp with her daughter Eva, she heard a great noise. It was the sound of an out-of-control wagon. So terrified were the mother and daughter that they bolted the cabin door and put a barricade in front of it. The noise continued, but it never got any closer and by the time August Parolin arrived, it had all but disappeared. Or so the story goes.[11]

As the area's lumber industry continued to grow, more settlers began to arrive, clearing the land for their small log shanties and stables, as well as for growing hay, oats, potatoes, turnips and any other vegetable that would take root.[12] On the rare occasion if there happened to be a surplus of crops, the homesteader had a ready market—namely the nearby lumber camps.

One of the earliest settlements to be established along the Pickerel River was Loring. Centrally located in the northern section of Parry Sound District, the tiny community was situated at the corner of where the four townships meet: McConkey, Hardy, Wilson and Mills. When travellers, arriving by boat along the Pickerel River as it flowed through McConkey Township, first spotted the settlement, it was nothing more than a small collection of shanties. The site was first called McConkey Corners, a name that stuck long after the post office was granted the official name of Loring.[13] As to why the name of Loring was eventually chosen, it appears that when the residents presented their MP, Conservative William Edward O'Brien of Thornhill, with a petition for a post office, he suggested naming it Loring, after his wife. At the age of fifty-two O'Brien had been elected to parliament on June 20, 1882, the same year he married a Miss Loring. Unfortunately, there is no record of her first name.[14] He held the District of Parry Sound for the Conservative Party until his defeat in 1896.[15]

Despite the shortage of standing timber in the region, lumbermen continued to cut down what they could. This photograph from the Pickerel River area shows very clearly that it took a considerable number of trees to make even this modest pile.

Records show that the very first people to settle McConkey Corners were brothers Robert and Andrew Arthur, who arrived sometime during the 1870s. Others to follow included Barney Fagan in 1880, then William and Henry Kirton, Johnston Currie, John Haggart and John Robertson. It wasn't long before more settlers appeared, this time in larger numbers—now only having to travel a short distance from Glenila to the south. Situated in Ferrie Township and first settled in 1875, Glenila proved a failure almost right from the start. But it was with optimism that pioneer Karl Ziehm provided the name of Glenila for the early post office. However, by the end of the first growing season, homesteaders realized the area's sandy soil was incapable of sustaining any type of crop. Unable to make a go of it, the last of its residents were gone before too many years passed, leaving the forest to swallow up the former community.[16]

Now, with new settlers arriving at Loring almost every day, two Scots related by marriage, John Haggart and John Robertson, set about building the first pit and skidway for whipsawing lumber to be used for floors, roofing material and doors in the homesteaders' shanties. Haggart, born in Glasgow in 1845, had married Robertson's sister, Janet Ann, before they immigrated to Canada. The two families settled at Loring in 1884. However, tragedy would strike the Haggart family in 1892 when Janet sustained unknown injuries and died from complications. Just forty-seven years of age, she left behind ten children, the three youngest having been born in Loring. Despite the difficulties and the struggles of the settlers, for the first few years at least, they persevered by walking the ninety-kilometre round trip to Dunchurch to obtain the necessary supplies. The men carried 100 pounds of supplies, the women, fifty pounds. But, by 1884 the circumstances changed dramatically for these residents, with not one, but two general stores in the works for Loring—courtesy of the Dunchurch merchants they had faithfully patronized earlier on.

Another Robertson, Robert, and his wife Betsy, a member of the Dobbs family of Golden Valley, seized the opportunity to open a store in the new settlement, and left their business interests in Dunchurch to move north. The couple purchased property on the northeast corner of where the four townships met in McConkey Corners. Paying John and Jane Sturdy $25 for their claim, the Robertsons not only built the first general store here, but a log boarding house as well. William and Dora Croswell, who were among the earlier settlers to the area, became the store managers and for a while the business flourished. At one point the boarding house was covered with lumber and whitewashed. From then on the locals referred to it as the White House. However, Robert and Betsy Robertson didn't remain in Loring for long, returning to Dunchurch in 1900. They sold their property to A.W. Sinclair and the store merchandise was purchased by Edmund Forsyth Sr.[17]

Following on the heels of the Robertson store, in 1885 the second Dunchurch merchant to open a store in Loring—it is said on the prompting of his mother—was Edward Kelcey. Edward was born on March 6, 1866, in Rugby, County of Warwickshire, England, to George Kelcey and Lucy Ann Mannering.[18] His father was a fairly well-off painter and decorator in Rugby, but when he contracted lead poisoning and given little chance for survival, the family immigrated to Canada in 1871. Securing about 150 acres of land surrounding the Narrows of Whitestone Lake through the Ontario Free Grants & Homestead Act, George built a steam-powered sawmill there, along with a general store and post office. Up until then the tiny settlement had been called Newcombe, but once the post office was established, George Kelcey is said to have renamed the community Dunchurch, after his wife's birthplace in England. In 1880, the Kelceys decided to send their two children back to Rugby to finish school. They returned to Canada in 1883. But just a year after Edward and his sister had settled back into a daily routine in Dunchurch, their father was mortally injured. On June 16, 1884, George had been cutting narrow flooring with a whirling saw when one of the strips caught the saw, flew off and struck him on the forehead, fracturing his skull and laying bare a portion of his brain. According to George Kelcey's obituary, "his last breath came at 9:00 p.m., with Dr. Campbell of McKellar in attendance."[19]

After her husband's death Lucy Ann Kelcey continued to operate the store with her son's help, but when she realized that the Robertsons had made a move to Loring to open a general store there, she urged Edward to follow suit. Edward Kelcey's first store was a two-storey log cabin and, as the story goes, the winter of 1885 was so cold that nails froze to the workmen's fingers during its construction. Although Kelcey's business officially opened on Christmas Day, Edward decided to hold a dance upstairs on New Year's Day to celebrate. Yes, it was still cold, and the fiddler is said to have put his arms around the stovepipe and played in that position for the entire dance.[20]

Edward eventually married in 1908. His bride was Lily Metcalfe of Toronto and the wedding took place in the city that September. His mother came to live with them in Loring, but later moved to California where, in 1933, she died at the age of 92.[21] Lily Kelcey died in 1941 at the age of 63, while Edward lived for another 21 years. His death came in 1962 at the age of 96. Both Lily and Edward are buried in Loring Cemetery.[22]

Just a stone's throw away from Loring was the waterfront settlement of Port Loring. However, after the post office was opened, both communities were referred to as "Loring" for the first few years at least. Port Loring was generally known as "Down at the Lake" Wauquimakog Lake (now Wilson Lake), meaning "lake surrounded by hardwood bush." The community's earliest recorded history suggests that incoming settlers were not interested in "waterfront" property except for catching a few fish. So in the very beginning, the only people using the area's waterways were either the Native people in their birchbark canoes, or lumbermen in their pointer boats. Due in part to the extensive number of lakes, rivers and small streams that served as transportation routes in Wilson Township, no actual roads were blazed into the area until years later. Because of its isolation, Port Loring's settlement stagnated, offering little more than a lone hotel and a few log shanties.

That remained the case until Donald Smith and Michael James Davis came along. In 1880, they were the first settlers to register their lands, and Davis' wife, Sarah Kirton, was reported to be the first white woman in Port Loring. Donald Smith was born August 31, 1844, at Duncan's Bay, Scotland. He immigrated to Canada in 1871, settling in Haldimand County and remaining there for seven years before moving north to Glenila, then to Port Loring. In 1881, he married a twenty-six-year-old Scottish lass, Barbara Rosie, in a wedding service held near Dunchurch.

When the Pickerel River took on greater importance in the lumbering business, the long peninsula between Wilson and Pigeon lakes was named Davis Point, after Michael Davis. The land was cleared of trees and seeded with grass to pasture logging company horses and was used for this purpose for many years.[23] As for Michael Davis, he was originally from Huron County, where he met and married Sarah Kirton on December 28, 1874, the service being held in a local Methodist church. His bride was to be one of five siblings to eventually settle in the Loring area.

Sarah, who was the oldest of the Kirton children, was born in England on January 1, 1849, and immigrated to Canada with her parents in 1853. James and Elizabeth Kirton would spend the first few years in Scarborough Township where their family grew to include Henry (b.1856), Hannah (b.1858), Mary (b.1860) and William (b.1862). The Kirtons' youngest daughter Mary would venture only as far north as Dunchurch, where she began teaching school. She married Wesley Wiley in Burk's Falls on June 30, 1887. When Henry Kirton arrived in Loring, he met and eventually married Margaret Avery. Hannah followed her brother in order to keep house for him but soon married herself on March 21, 1887. The groom was James Boyd. However, not long after setting up their households, brother and sister found themselves taking care of other people's children. That practice would happen far too many times in those days, as when a wife died leaving children to care for, the husband often called upon the neighbours to help out. When John VanEvery's wife died, the four boys were taken in by Henry and Margaret until John left for the Prairies. The youngest of the VanEvery children, Owen Herbert, remained with them and was eventually adopted by the couple. Hannah and James, in the meantime, took in

John and Annie Currie to raise as their own. The couple left Loring in 1920 and moved south. James died in Waterloo on February 18, 1936, Hannah, on October 15, 1945, in Toronto.[24]

Although the Kirtons' youngest son William lived in Dunchurch for a while, taking up blacksmithing for George Kelcey when he married Minnie Delphine Gorham on July 8, 1885, he moved closer to the rest of his family. His bride was the daughter of Thomas Jasper and Sarah Ann (Coon) Gorham of Lima, Allan County, Ohio. When the couple first arrived north, William staked his claim on Lots 30 and 31, Concession 12 in Mills Township. However, it soon dawned on them that living so far away from the community meant William would have a difficult time in attracting customers. He eventually sold the property to Johnston Currie in order to move into Loring. The Kirtons settled on land they bought from Barney Fagan. Ideally situated, the property included a shanty built by Fagan where William and Minnie lived until they could afford to build a bigger house and blacksmith shop. Besides blacksmithing, William also farmed and ran a small general store.[25]

In all, William and Minnie Kirton had eight children, William Jr. (b. April 21, 1887–d. November 1950), Margaret May (b. January 6, 1891–d. July 26, 1927), Everett (b. March 27, 1894–1984), Ida Laurena (b. December 20, 1896), Jasper Earle (b. December 20, 1898), John Lawrence (b. September 5, 1900), Francis Archie (b. June 24, 1905) and Eva Lillian (b. May 11, 1908). It is fortunate that William Kirton's second eldest son Everett took such an interest in the

Everett Kirton was barely in his twenties when he started navigating along the Pickerel River in his small boat, enjoying the spectacular wilderness. Going to work at Lost Channel as the agent for the Key Valley Railway line, he would witness first-hand the rise and fall of this bush community of 1,000. His last time out on the river in the late 1970s, when he was an old man, shocked him—Lost Channel had completely disappeared.

early days of Port Loring. His unpublished memoirs, particularly those describing Lost Channel, remain the only recorded accounts of the area to survive to the present day.

Everett's writings on the history of the communities in northern Parry Sound District are now the property of the Nipissing Township Museum. In reading them, one learns that his greatest pleasure as a child was sitting together with the old-timers—the area's first settlers. Everett listened intently as the men recalled their days in the logging industry, and would write it all down later. Although never a river driver himself, while growing up Everett worked most of the jobs available in both the small and large logging camps. His closest brush with a river drive was the summer he operated a gas-powered boat on a drive on the Key River near Key Harbour. And while Everett worked in the logging camps, sawmills and later tourist camps, his father William who was well into his fifties started work as a blacksmith at the mill at Lost Channel.

During the Spanish Flu pandemic in the late fall of 1918, William Kirton contracted pneumonia. He is believed to have died in the makeshift hospital set up by the Schroeder Mills and Timber Company, although there are some references suggesting that his death came at the beginning of the New Year while in hospital in Parry Sound.[26]

Everett was to marry Elma Ward of St. Thomas in 1927, but just three years later he was mourning the death of another parent, his mother, Minnie. By the time he'd earned his scaling licence in 1938 the logging industry was almost nearing the end, so he went on to teach school and for a time clerked in one of the local general stores. It was during this time that Everett and Elma raised two boys, Glenn and Carl. The family moved to Powassan in 1949 at which time Everett became the division clerk for the Department of Lands and Forests. At this point, already middle-aged, he began recording community histories, township by township.[27] Everett kept up his writing long after he retired in March of 1964.

At the age of eighty-two Everett Kirton climbed into a motor boat and took what would be

Courtesy of Glenn Kirton

In 1949, at the age of 55, Everett Kirton and his wife moved from Loring to Powassan, where he took up the position of division clerk, as pictured here, for the Department of Lands and Forests. When Everett retired in March 1964, he began writing down his memories of the early days of settlement and logging around Pickerel River.

his last trip down the Pickerel River. The year was 1976. His intention was, so he said, to travel from Port Loring through to Dollars Dam, to explore all the bays, channels and islands of his youth. Everett wrote down what he observed, but what he remembered as a long, unbroken forest shoreline was now dotted by cottages. Although the new development came as a pleasant surprise to him, he was in for a shock once his motor boat reached Lost Channel. The village was completely gone—swallowed up by a vast growth of poplar and white birch. Not a trace was left of the sawmill, the lumber company offices, the storehouses or for that matter, the general store, the cookery and the sleeping quarters of the loggers. As for the rental homes of the sawmill workers and their families, they too were gone. For Everett, his recollections of the community harkened back to the glory years between the end of the First World War and the 1920s when he worked at Lost Channel. At that time the area had a population of over 1,000 with a busy steamboat business that plied the seventy-kilometre route between Port Loring and the railhead.

Lost Channel grew out of the wilderness and became a busy little village in a very short time. Its demise it seems was equally as fast. "I felt so sad after looking at it that I did not get out of the boat, but slowly and sadly turned the boat around, and without a backward look, left the scene where I had spent many of the happiest years of my life. A place where I worked hard and enjoyed it, met many people who became my dearest friends. Where every day had been like a little bit of heaven. Goodbye Lost Channel," wrote Everett Kirton, on June 1, 1977.[28]

Lost Channel: A Company Town

McConkey Corners/Loring wasn't the only community to flourish in the northern part of the Parry Sound District. While the lumberjacks engaged in clearing the forests for the various lumber companies, the area surrounding the Pickerel River and the railhead at Lost Channel deservedly earned the reputation of being the busiest during the fifty-year pine-logging era that was to follow. In the summer of 1893, a reporter with the *Parry Sound North Star* recorded a "tell-all" statement made by John Armstrong, logging contractor for the Ontario Lumber Company, "There's a full 200,000,000 board feet of logs in the river this year." Armstrong was referring to the company's river drive from Restoule River down the French to Georgian Bay.

There are two versions of the story on how Lost Channel got its name. One as told by Dob Walton in his memoirs of the family's boat-building business at Loring and the other in the recollections of area old-timer Everett Kirton. Both explanations involve a river drive down the Pickerel River but that's where the similarities end. In the Walton memoirs, the story tells of a log boom with the river drivers led by OLC's walking boss Black Jack Kennedy being blown off course. On that fateful day, the crew was met with gale force winds at the "Elbow," the point where the Pickerel River turns north towards Dollars Lake. It forced the entire crew deep into the recesses of a three-kilometre long channel. The men remained "lost" in that channel for about three weeks, recalls Walton, waiting for the wind to change direction so that they could get back out into the main river.

In the second story as told by Everett Kirton, the walking boss for this particular river drive remains unnamed and was supposedly a replacement for the regular boss at Wilson Dam. Although Kirton states he was informed that the original walking boss on the drive was well-liked and his men would do what they could to make things run smoothly, on this particular drive, the new man was given an entirely different reception. As it turned out, he was a complete stranger to the river, but since he was in charge, he instructed the crew to follow his orders, So they did exactly that. Instead of turning towards Dollars Lake at the Elbow as they usually did, the river drivers kept the boom going in a westerly direction until they ran out of water. It was

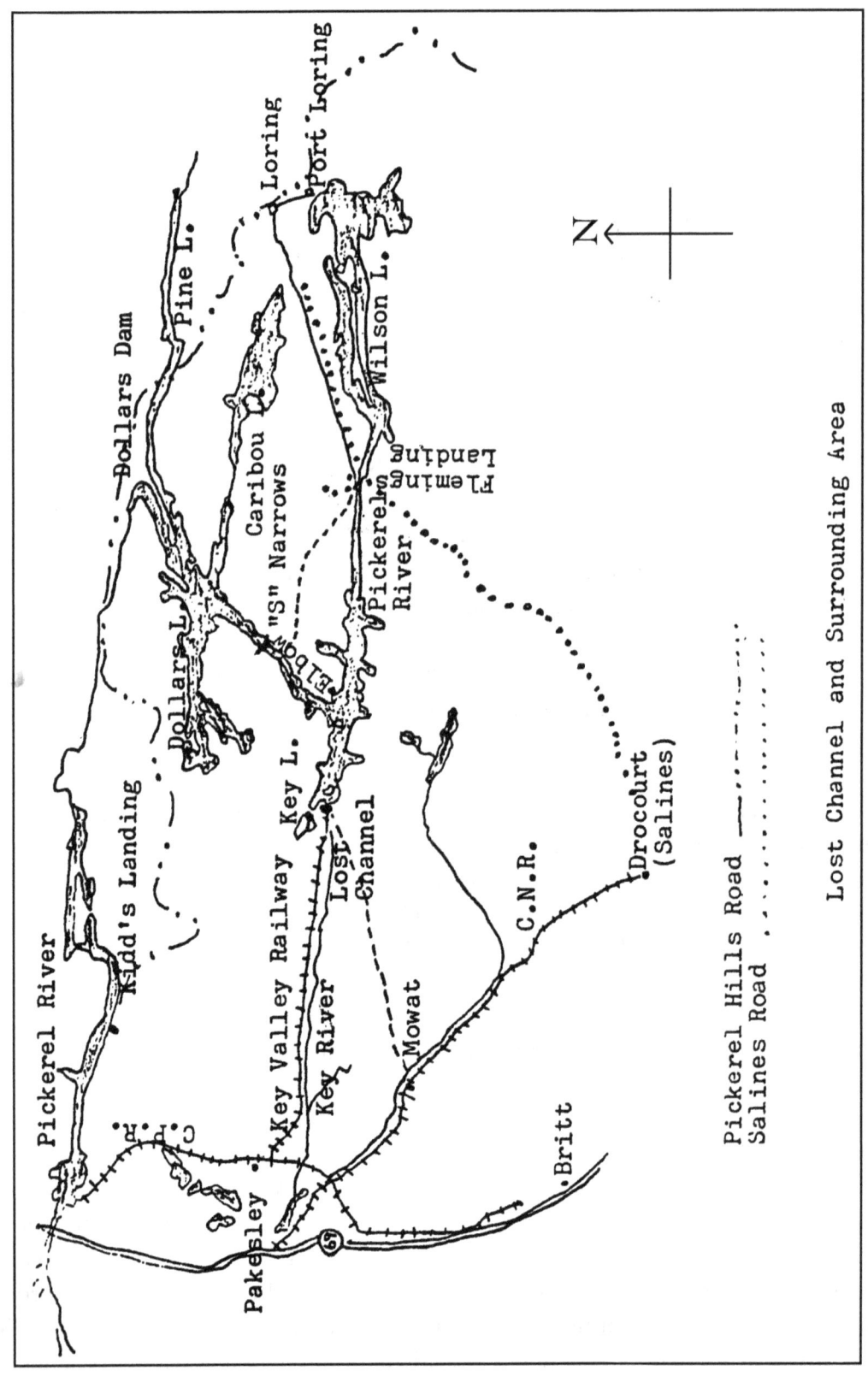

only then that it dawned on the man that he should have ordered the boom turned sharply to the right at the Elbow. Kirton adds in his recollections that none of the river drivers ever let on how the boom chains came loose once they reached the dead end, letting all the logs drift onto shore. The end result was the loss of over two months of driving weather to gather all the logs together into a new boom, and "warp" back the three kilometres to the Elbow.[1]

But it was here, deep in the recesses of the Lost Channel where the village site was eventually hacked out of the rock. Situated about forty kilometres northeast of the Town of Parry Sound, the community of Lost Channel was created by the Lauder, Spears and Howland Lumber Company in 1910. It is interesting to note that long before Lucien B. Howland was made a partner in the company, James Lauder and Joseph Spears were seasoned lumbermen, heavily involved in a number of sawmills, including ones in Blind River along the north shore of Lake Superior and in Wilberforce in the Haliburton area. There is also some suggestion that the partners had interests in a Toronto lumberyard.[2] Although there is no evidence to prove which Toronto lumberyard Lauder and Spears were involved with, there are only two choices—it was either the giant Elias Rogers Coal and Lumber Company or the yard belonging to Reid and Company. Both were located by the waterfront at the busy corner of The Esplanade and Berkeley Street in the heart of old Toronto.[3]

Joseph Spears, who originally settled in Burk's Falls before deciding to head north, ran his own private lumbering operation for a time at Horn Lake, just north of the village. But, by 1912, Lauder and Spears had enough money to buy a timber limit in Mowat Township. Having contracted the milling of some of the sawlogs to Cole's Mill on Key Lake, they had the lumber hauled by teams of horses along Coles Road to the railway at Mowat Station. From here it was shipped out to various destinations. W.H. Cole and Sons were in operation from about 1912 to 1920.

However, at the same time that lumberjacks were cutting logs for Lauder and Spears, the Victoria Harbour Lumber Company was also cutting white pine on its limits surrounding Dollars Lake. Lauder and Spears wanted the licence and, eventually, the pair acquired it but at a great cost to them. Within just two years, however, their financial situation seemed to improve somewhat as a third partner, none other than civil engineer Lucien B. Howland, took an interest in the company. Since all three men had dealings with the Wilberforce sawmill and were well-acquainted with each other, Lauder and Spears jumped at Howland's offer to finance the new company. The only condition was that Lucien Howland wanted to be a full partner.[4]

Finding the money wasn't a problem for Lucien as his father-in-law, Charles J. Pusey, was a railway contractor, building railways in eastern Ontario as well as in Mexico. However, the end result was that instead of contracting to other local mills as Lauder and Spears intended, Howland decided instead to build a company sawmill. Joseph Spears found out about his partner's intentions quite by accident. One day late in the winter of 1916 as he was dealing with personal matters at Mowat Station, a whole trainload of sawmill machinery was shunted off at the railway siding. To his shock, he was informed by the station attendant that the shipment was intended for the new sawmill of Lauder, Spears and Howland. The only problem was—there was no new sawmill—at least not yet. Not long after the machinery arrived, the site for the new mill

In the early days, logging camps were scattered all along the Pickerel River system, some larger than others. The background of this rare photograph shows a typical lumber camp with a cookhouse, a bunkhouse, a foreman's cabin, some stables and a blacksmith's shop. Moored at the waterfront are the "cabooses" of the river drivers, those floating campsites that followed the large booms down the river to Georgian Bay.

was literally blown up out of the bedrock and pine trees, and Lost Channel was born.[5] It is said that the boilers and most of the machinery for this mill was hauled by horse-drawn sleighs over an ice road, nine kilometres from Mowat Station.[6]

Everett Kirton worked at Lost Channel during its boom years. As noted earlier, what we know about what life was like in this company town comes from his recollections, recorded years later. Everett remembered that the construction of Howland's large sawmill began in 1917, about the same time as the lumber company's men began streaming in. A cookery and a bunkhouse were constructed for the men, along with stables for the company horses. To encourage settlement and attract skilled workers, the Lauder, Spears and Howland Lumber Company built a number of houses for the families of their mill workers.[7] Joseph Spears personally saw to it that Lost Channel had a public school so that the children of the mill's employees would get an education.

Crystal Cameron (later Mrs. James LaBrash of Golden Valley) became the first teacher. She was not only hired by the lumber company, but her salary paid by it as well. The very first classes were held in one of the mill's offices. During the heyday of the village, there were as many as twenty-three students attending the school. The children brought scribblers to class and Spears arranged for a small blackboard and chalk for the teacher. The community even had its own newspaper for a while, the *Lost Channel Blabber*. Only a few copies of each edition were handprinted, and they were passed from one villager to another. Its only editor, whose name has been lost to history, is quoted in one edition as saying, "Yes, we are back in the bush all right. We are so far back we don't even know there is a war going on."[8]

For the 23-year-old Everett Kirton, once the sawmill at Lost Channel was completed, it was the most efficient operation he had ever seen. Powered by a big steam engine, the flywheel, according to Kirton's estimation, was at least sixteen feet in diameter, and the leather drive belt was about two feet wide and a hundred feet long—endless with no splices. There were three massive boilers, eight feet in diameter and sixteen feet or more long. The fireboxes under the boilers were huge and the fuel was mostly sawdust from the mill saws. As he explained it, "The sawdust was fed into the fireboxes by means of conveyors, which came directly from underneath the saw, and which could be regulated to just put the right amount of sawdust into the fireboxes."

The main mill building at Lost Channel was three storeys, with the bottom level containing the slush chains (sawdust conveyors), the driveshaft, pulleys and belts that drove the machinery above. The second floor was where the lumber itself was processed. In Kirton's words, "The jack-ladder—an endless chain in a trough—carried the sawlogs from the waters of Lost Channel and entered the centre of the sawmill, facing the water. These logs were mechanically kicked off the jack-ladder when they reached the top. Some logs were kicked off to one side and the rest

Logjams on the Magnetawan River were quite a common occurrence. In this postcard of a logjam at Byng Inlet, one gets a sense of how large some of these jams could become. Sometimes many thousands of logs would be collected, so tightly squeezed together that water could not pass through them. This pile of logs would be right to the bottom of the river. Opening up a logjam was a tricky business, with many a river driver losing his life, to lie buried in an unmarked grave along the Magnetawan River.

to the other side of the mill. At the one side, close to the jack-ladder were two circular saws set about eight inches apart. As the log was conveyed lengthwise between these saws, a slab was cut off each side. The flattened logs were then turned over on one side and passed through a set of many saws, called a gangsaw, and they came out of this all made into lumber." As for the top floor, it contained a small space that was used as a filing room where the saws were sharpened.

Everett Kirton remembers the mill running ten hours a day, six days a week and credits the millwrights and machinists for keeping it in perfect working order. It meant that about 2,200 logs went up the jack-ladder into the mill on a daily basis, with around 140,000 board feet of pine lumber coming out of the other end of the mill each day. Some of the mill families included the following: Malowney, Stamp, Charlebois, Carey and McCastle. Dane Rutherford was the bookkeeper, Norman McCastle was the barber and George Carey cooked for the mill gang.[9]

It was most unfortunate that Lost Channel's fleeting prosperity was to come at the tail end of the region's golden lumbering era. By the time the Lauder, Spears and Howland Lumber Company completed the building of the town, a number of other area lumber companies had already begun their downward spiral, a trend that was becoming evident as far back as 1910. With virtually no pine stands left on their limits, some company officials chose to sell their claims while others abandoned their rights completely.

The Ontario Lumber Company was forced into bankruptcy as a result of having to pay heavy fines for dumping excess sawdust into the area's waterways—however, not before the company's massive timber limits had grown to include most of McConkey Township, and parts of Hardy, Mills and Ferrie townships. As was to be the case many times over, when a lumber company failed, there was always another one waiting in the wings to take its place. Pine Lake Lumber eventually purchased OLC's massive sawmill, dismantling it and later relocating it to Pickerel Landing Village.[10] While the Pine Lake Lumber Company bought out OLC, the Parry Sound Lumber Company continued to operate in the south half of McConkey Township. The American firm of Holt Timber Company bought the McKenzie Township limits from Graves and Bigwood, and then constructed a logging rail line to haul cut logs to Big Deer Lake. The railway, about ten kilometres in length, saved the company valuable time in getting the logs to the Magnetawan River, where they were then boomed down to Georgian Bay. Limits in a small section of Wilson Township belonging to the Manley Chew Bros. of Midland were eventually bought out by the McGibbon Lumber Company of Penetang.[11]

By the time the last of the large American lumber companies, Schroeder Mills and Timber Company of Milwaukee, Wisconsin, started up its Canadian operations in 1913, it had already acquired timber holdings in Brown, Wilson and Ferrie townships. Was it strategy, or just plain luck that four years later, in 1917, Schroeder Mills was able to purchase most of the timber rights in Blair Township, which included one of the last stands of virgin pine left in the region? Only time would tell, as the Lauder, Spears and Howland Lumber Company also held timber rights in Blair Township as well as their sawmill at Lost Channel.[12] During the winter months, the sawmill at Lost Channel was shut down and many of the mill workers headed for the Schroeder lumber camps upriver. According to Everett Kirton, it meant that

During the winter months, the sawmill at Lost Channel was shut down, and many of the mill workers headed for the Schroeder Mill and Timber Company's lumber camps upriver. Pictured here in this postcard is a large group of lumberjacks with their teams in front of the camp's main buildings. It must have been an important visit, as a well-dressed young couple with a small child is seated in the horse-drawn sleigh, centre left in the picture.

the skeleton crew remaining behind to make repairs at the mill had to come up with scaled back social activities.

One of the busiest homes at Lost Channel during this time was that of Bert Laughlin and his family. During his many visits, Kirton explains, to pass the time, guests listened to the Victrola, played cards with the Laughlin daughters, Edith and Gertie, and told jokes. Gertie was married to the mill's bookkeeper, Dane Rutherford. Everyone in this household was always talking at once, remembers Kirton. Another home that enjoyed numerous visits from the mill workers was that of Irishman John Ennis. His wife and daughter Florence also enjoyed playing cards, but visits were cut short by the fact that John Ennis went to bed at nine o'clock in the evening.[13]

One of the most entertaining households at Lost Channel was that of Andre Charlebois. Things sometimes got so boisterous that Charlebois would threaten to throw everyone out—that is until his eldest daughters, Bernadette and Pauline, would whisper into their Papa's ear that the racket would stop if he allowed the guests to stay. Kirton recalls that on numerous occasions the evening would end with a square dance as there was always at least a couple of guests on hand who owned either a violin or mouth organ. "Calling the changes in those square dances was done by turns and it really was more fun than dancing to a professional caller," wrote Kirton. "It was usually the outlandish hour of 10:30 p.m. when we bid the Charlebois family adieu, and we all started home, each dropping off at his or her home as we went past it, until only one would be left to walk the last short way home."

The "Jitney," pictured here, was a one-ton Model T Ford truck with flanged wheels that travelled from Pakesley to Lost Channel over the Key Valley Railway line. Board seats ran along the inside of the truck, accommodating upwards of twelve passengers. Moving at speeds between ten and eighteen kilometres per hour, the Jitney carried its own turntable so that it could turn around at the end of each run.

For Everett Kirton, Lost Channel was very busy—for a one-industry town. Yes, it had just the one sawmill, owned by Lauder, Spears and Howland, and everything else was company owned as well. But work was available year-round with regular pay and the inhabitants created their own amusements, whether it was simply fishing, boating, family picnics or the few dances in the company-built dance hall. Kirton remembers that the general store had reasonable prices, with Harkie Haggart of Loring making the trip to Lost Channel twice a week during the summer months, to sell fresh vegetables and meat to the mill cookery and store.[14]

Despite the high optimism, the summer of 1918 would be the last of the good times for Lauder, Spears and Howland Lumber Company. That year the mill at Lost Channel was producing about ten million board feet of lumber. Although half of it was already "in pile," the balance was being cut at the rate of a million board feet per week. The price of lumber was also increasing, averaging $30 per thousand board feet. It meant that the company's seasonal cut was now worth $300,000. However, Lauder, Spears and Howland were heavily in debt because of their involvement with the Key Valley Railway that eventually would connect Lost Channel to Pakesley, a station on the Canadian Pacific Railway line. Begun in 1914, in just three years the construction of the twenty kilometres of railway had already cost the company close to six times the original estimate. The Key Valley Railway was named for the narrow valley through which the rail bed was cut. Employing a largely immigrant workforce, mainly Italian, the company had the large rocks at Lost Channel blasted out to make way for the railway line.[15] The work was desperately tough and slow going.

In 1918, one last push was made by the lumber company to obtain funds to complete milling the last of the season's timber haul. While the partners waited for word from the bank, it was decided that a diversion was needed, hence a large new bunkhouse was built for the mill workers. To celebrate the occasion, a dance was held with everyone welcomed. Word spread fast and the curious came from far and near to see what all the fuss was about. People came from not only the Town of Parry Sound but the Pickerel River Indian Reserve, as well as all points between Port Loring and Trout Creek. Well-heeled guests from Courtney's Kawigamog Lodge also attended, Everyone was reported to have had a good time, dancing until dawn, with a monumental breakfast served up at the cookery.[16]

Impending financial ruin, however, would be the least of the lumber company's worries as the Spanish Influenza pandemic of 1918–19 finally spread to the most remote areas of the district. Lost Channel's schoolteacher Crystal Cameron, along with Muriel Stamp, were the only two women who were not stricken. Afraid to leave for fear of spreading the disease, the women remained in the village to assist the only physician, a Dr. Clee who is said to have used a number of home remedies to treat the ill. Those who were strong enough were transported by train to hospitals in Parry Sound and Sudbury. The influenza also hit Schroeder Mills and Timber Company's logging camps and at first the seriously ill were removed and taken to Lost Channel for treatment. However, there were no hospital facilities, or even a doctor in their midst to care for so many desperately sick men, and the surrounding lumber camps didn't want the infected in their midst either. Finally, the head office of Schroeder Mills and Timber Company stepped in to set up a temporary hospital. Located in the woods far away from the village, this makeshift hospital (21 x 23 metres) had one-ply rough lumber boards tacked to poles to serve as a floor, with walls two-boards high. A tent was pitched over the top to serve as a roof. Homemade bunks with a little hay and rough, grey blankets served as hospital cots. A wood stove was set up in one corner.[17] Word had it that no germs ever found their way out of that hospital.

The nursing staff consisted of one young man who had no previous nursing experience. He remained on site seven days a week, around the clock, with food being brought in from a nearby camp cookery. So feared was the disease that attempts to take one dying mill worker, by the name of Guy Cook, back to Port Loring was thwarted at the docks. Fred Hampel had travelled to Lost Channel to take the man home. However, once they arrived at Port Loring, they were not allowed to get out disembark. Cook died the next day, back at Lost Channel. It was November 11, 1918, the day the Great War would be declared over. For residents of Lost Channel battling the outbreak of influenza, it wasn't until November 12 that the mill whistle was finally blown by Carmen Spears, the five-year-old son of Joseph Spears, to mark the end of the war.[18]

A number of lumberjacks and mill workers were to die of the Spanish Flu. The carpenter and his helper were kept busy building rough coffins to bury the dead. Those who died at the camp hospital with no known relatives were given a simple burial nearby. A chapter from the Bible was read over the deceased, followed by a short prayer commending the soul of the departed to his God.[19] The weather conditions in the fall of 1918 could have very easily precipitated the influenza epidemic. There was a continuous downpour of rain, day in and day out, occasionally mixed with wet snow. Due to the heavy rains, hay could not be harvested and the lumber camps couldn't get their quotas before freeze-up. Ice on the Pickerel River froze only a couple of inches before the snow fell, preventing any further ice buildup. With the camps nearly out of hay and not enough ice formed on the river to haul whatever hay was available, something needed to be done. As Everett Kirton recalls, a team of ten to twelve lumberjacks got in front of a V-shaped snowplough to make a passable road along the riverbank to Lost Channel. It was a ten-kilometre trip each way. The company walking boss sent the men to do the job, not the horses, because horses cost money and could slip into the river and perish.[20]

The Lauder, Spears and Howland Lumber Company was teetering on the brink of disaster, and only a few months into the new year it was finally all over. The chain of events leading to the bank's refusal to extend any more credit to the company but instead calling in a sizable portion of the loan within thirty days, remains shrouded in mystery. There is some speculation that the head office of the Schroeder Mills and Timber Company sent someone to intercept the bank representative as he was on his way to meet Lauder and Spears.[21] The American company official supposedly made his proposal to the banker at the Pakesley Railway Station. Schroeder Mills would assume Lauder, Spears and Howland's bank loan in exchange for the company's assets, which were held by the bank as collateral. When word finally reached James Lauder, Joseph Spears and Lucien Howland as to what had happened, the partners made one last effort to raise the money by contacting financial houses in Toronto and Montreal. It was too late. As a result, in 1919, the whole Village of Lost Channel was dropped by the bank into the waiting arms of the Schroeder Mills and Timber Company, including the Key Valley Railway and all of the Lauder, Spears and Howland Company timber limits. Adding insult to injury, Joseph Spears and his family were ordered to leave their palatial home. In later years, Joseph Spears would often comment that "If the bank had only stayed with us another five or six weeks until the logs were all cut, the increase in the price of lumber would have offset the amount we sank into the railway."[22]

In no time at all, the American-based company completed the standard gauge railway to Pakesley, built a lumberyard there and installed a water tank for watering the company's five locomotives. Although most of the families who had worked for Lauder, Spears and Howland left when Schroeder Mills took over, it wasn't long before a new population had moved in, eager to help expand the mill and bush operations.

By the early 1920s there were more than 1,000 people living and working at Lost Channel. On the land directly across the small bay from the sawmill, a spur line was constructed to connect with the Key Valley Railway line, a dock built and a hotel established, run by Oliver Dixon. Now, any lumber brought to Lost Channel by scows from upriver could be loaded onto railway cars without interfering with the sawmill's operation.[23]

To look after the company's interests in the area, the absentee owners wisely engaged James Ludgate of Parry Sound as their general manager at Lost Channel.[24] Referred to as a "local bull of the woods," James Ludgate was truly a veteran lumberman by the time he went to work for the American company. Other Ludgate family members who would be employed by the Schroeder Mills and Timber Company included James Ludgate Sr., as general manager, and Douglas Ludgate, manager for the Key Valley Railway.[25] In time, James Ludgate would put in five camps and begin floating millions of board feet of sawlogs down the Magnetawan and Still rivers on an annual basis.[26] He also also built a medium-sized sawmill at the junction of the Big and Little Key rivers on the rail line shortly after its completion. Here, logs cut nearby were milled into lumber. This mill continued operations until 1930.

In fact, a number of smaller sawmills sprang up along the Pickerel River during this period. The lumber processed was, for the most part, loaded onto scows and towed to Lost Channel to be transported out by rail to the Pakesley station.[27] Schroeder Mills did locate one of its logging camps close to the Key Valley rail line. Situated about one kilometre east of Pakesley, it was put into operation shortly after the company acquired Lost Channel. Over the next five years, logs cut by the men at this camp were dumped into the Key River and floated down to Key Harbour, then towed by lake tugs to Victoria Harbour for processing.

Interestingly enough, only twenty years earlier the Ludgates had been involved in their own lumber company, having acquired large tracts of standing timber along J.R. Booth's railway line (Ottawa, Arnprior & Parry Sound Railway) through Christie Township. Soon, the family would "own" its very own little community. When the railway built a small flag stop and siding, naming it Maple Lake Station, it was a relatively obscure spot sandwiched between the Edgington and Beatty stations west of Seguin Falls in the southwest corner of Parry Sound District. The Ludgates seized the opportunity to begin construction here. First, they built a general store located just south of the railway tracks, followed by three homes for its lumber company workers— all of whom happened to be members of the Percy D. Sword family. Although the Ludgate Lumber Company continued logging the southernwestern corner of the Parry Sound District, by 1900 it had sold off all its interests at Maple Lake Station to the Sword family and several of the Ludgates moved on.

However, more Sword family members put money into the existing housing stock. By 1904 a school was built for the area's children, and later the Maple Lake Hotel, run by John and Annie Sword, would appear in the community. John Sword became the owner of the old general store, with Thomas Sword appointed as the store manager. Before much time had lapsed the community's name was changed from Maple Lake Station to Swords. It is interesting to note that Thomas Sword ran the family's little general store until his death in 1923.[28]

The Last Stands

By 1915 the lumber companies were finally beginning to come to terms with the prospects that supplies of standing pine would not last much longer. After such a promising start to the industry, it was hard to believe that just fifty years later, the Dokis Reserve and the Schroeder Mills and Timber Company licence in Blair Township represented the last two stands of pine left to be logged in northern Parry Sound District. As for the remnants of standing timber remaining in a few inaccessible spots, lumbermen felt it wasn't worth the cost to harvest. Everett Kirton remembers that the Indian reserve, comprising much of the northern sections of Hardy and McConkey townships bordering on the French River, as well as a large island in the French River below the Chaudière Dam, was once covered by dense forest of virgin pine.[1]

In the early 1910s, the area's logging industry got one final boost from the Ontario government, as it surveyed the Dokis Reserve into sections, or berths as they were called in those days, and put the timber rights up for sale. Lumber companies whose bids were successful included that of Manley Chew of Midland, the Long Lake Co., the Georgian Bay Co. the Hettler Co. and the one belonging to J.B. Smith. The money collected by the government as timber dues was supposedly placed in a trust fund for the Reserve. However, no one knows for sure if this was ever done as records are sketchy at best. As for these latter logging operations, they would only last another fifteen years before the last of the timber ran out.[2]

A few lumber companies would turn to harvesting birch and hemlock. True, the wood was heavier and harder to handle than the pine and the processed lumber not as valuable, but it was just about all that was left. The first to harvest the secondary timber was the Bruce and Kirk Lumber Company, belonging to George Bruce and a Mr. Kirk. A medium-sized sawmill was built on a little bay named Bruce's Bay, on the Pickerel River near Lost Channel. At first the company had its own winter logging camps. Later, they would rely on the area's settlers to cut the logs on their own land and haul them either straight to the Pickerel River, or its tributaries, the Wolf River or Caribou Creek.[3]

Other lumbermen to join Bruce and Kirk in harvesting birch and hemlock were Arthur Empey and Albert Brunne. Empey first built a sawmill on Toad Lake, part of the Pickerel River

By the first decade of the 20th century, lumber companies were becoming desperate in their search for marketable pine in leftover timber stands. As can be seen in this early photograph, clear-cutting the bush around the Pickerel River was producing a very different kind of harvest. The bulk of the trees cut are small in diameter, and what has been left standing is smaller still.

waterway, later moving the mill to Long Lake, southeast of Arnstein. He would move the mill one more time, this time to Stanley Lake, south of Golden Valley, to be closer to his suppliers. Brunne on the other hand settled for a mill site on Wilson Lake at Port Loring. Both lumbermen relied mostly on timber cut by the settlers on their own lots.[4] All the lumber processed by the two mills was eventually transported by scows to Lost Channel where it was loaded onto box cars and shipped over the Key Valley Railway to Pakesley.

Following its acquisition of Lost Channel and all its assets from a bankrupted Lauder, Spears and Howland Lumber Company, the Schroeder Mills and Timber Company established a lumberyard at Pakesley on the Canadian Pacific Railway line. It was from here that the company shipped to its markets in Toronto, Detroit, Chicago and New York. Schroeder Mills also built a water tank at Pakesley to provide water for its five locomotives, along with a coal dock, two bunkhouses, two office buildings, a boarding house and stables for horses. To ensure that there was an adequate food supply for travellers, the company also set up a root house for vegetables plus an ice house. With the majority of lumber from the area passing through the Pakesley Station, eventually a general store, post office, restaurant and hotel were established, along with a fire-ranger station.[5] When William Crozier took over as station agent at Pakesley around 1919, he had to make do with an existing portable station. This building could be loaded on a flat car and taken where ever it was needed. But by 1924 the population of Pakesley had grown to 150 and with an increase in the number of travellers passing through, the CPR built a permanent railway station with a concrete basement and seven rooms spacious enough to accommodate the station agent and his family.[6]

At first the prospects seemed good for the settlement at Pakesley but less than ten years later, Lost Channel was no longer in business. When Schroeder Mills and Timber Company took over, it immediately set about to build four bunkhouses for its single mill workers. By the mid-1920s an additional thirty-five homes were constructed at Lost Channel to house the mill employees and their families. A new school was established, along with a hospital, dance hall and company store.[7] At that time Lost Channel had the largest operating sawmill in the area, along with a community population of 300. The residents even had electrical power. But the reality was about to set in. Time had run out on harvesting what was left of the area's standing pine and John Schroeder knew it.[8] By the time the mill shut down, a domino effect had begun in the region. The residents would never recover. The lumberyard at Pakesley still contained forty million running board feet of lumber, all of which had to be sold at reduced prices. The first-grade dried lumber was sold in job lots for garage and barn construction at bargain prices. Hardwood slatting was sold at 50 cents a cord for locomotive fuel.

In 1926, the Schroeder Mills and Timber Company's head office decided to sell the mill at Lost Channel and accepted an offer from George Bruce, of Bruce and Kirk Lumber Company. Taking James Playfair of Victoria Harbour on as his business partner, Bruce would name the new venture the Pakesley Lumber Company.[9] Switching over from white pine to hemlock, spruce and jack pine, the company made a go of it at first, shipping over 150,000 board feet per day from September to December. John Schroeder wisely chose to remain in control of the Key Valley Railway to reap the financial benefits to be gleaned there.[10] But Bruce and Playfair had their hands full as the mill was old and most of the machinery had worn out. Attempting to cut hardwood logs created all sorts of problems. Instead of the resinous pine sawdust that had burned so readily in the fire boxes under the steam boilers, there was now water-soaked birch and hemlock sawdust that put the fires out as quickly as they were started. Then, on November 1, 1930, disaster would strike. A fire from an undetermined source broke out in the rail shop and quickly spread to the mill, burning it to the ground. Although the insurance company settled and George Bruce managed to rebuild the mill on a smaller scale before the new timber season, a few years later he died unexpectedly. Playfair is believed to have gone to Midland, as investors were withdrawing their money. In 1933, the mill closed down for good and the last of the residents were gone by 1936.

Just a year later, on May 25, 1937, James Playfair would die at the age of seventy-six. The sawmill at Lost Channel was dismantled, and it, along with the railway equipment, including sixty flatbed cars and a quantity of steel tracks, was sold. The abandoned right-of-way was turned into a truck road.[11] At the other end of the railway, although the Department of Lands and Forests continued to maintain its ranger station until about 1958, by then the streets of Pakesley were almost deserted. The hotel and post office were both closed down in 1950 and the railway station torn down by the CPR in 1971. It wouldn't be until 1976 that a bridge was constructed over the Pickerel River at the S-Narrows and Highway #522 extended through to Highway #69, using the Key Valley right-of-way as part of it.[12]

With only one industry, logging, the "Hungry Thirties" would have a devastating effect on a number of the settlements along the Pickerel River. With the demise of Lost Channel, Everett Kirton remembered all too clearly that without work, there was no money and little in the way of any government assistance. It wasn't long before many of the inhabitants fell on hard times. For the few remaining businesses, it became a struggle to survive. Cecil T. Kidd, who operated the general store in Port Loring and was also the postmaster, devised a plan to start buying sawlogs from the farmers. He had them milled at Brunne's sawmill, then shipped the lumber out to be sold for whatever money he could get for it. Although prices had hit rock bottom during the 1930s, it was a lifesaver for the residents who now had some money, however little, to pay for goods purchased at Kidd's general store.[13]

The golden era of logging may have come to an end, but many still saw the region as a hunter's paradise. When the Schroeder limits were finally all logged out, some of the company's abandoned camp sites were grabbed up by hunting clubs from down south. Deer were always plentiful, and today the area's wilderness habitat continues to support large herds. About 10,000 white-tailed deer, the largest herd in Ontario, make the Loring Deer Yard their winter home. But if one happens to be hiking through the area, particularly near Lost Channel, stop and listen closely. It's not deer you might hear, but something totally unexpected. Grunting—real or imagined? In days gone by the grunts and squeals of pigs, yes, pigs, could be heard all over the Channel. It was the practice of the inhabitants of Lost Channel to let loose a great many pigs every spring. The swine lived on scraps from the cookhouse and whatever else they could scrounge. Then in the fall, the pigs were rounded up and slaughtered for meat for the lumber camps.[14] Take a walk sometime, and decide for yourself what it is you might hear!

10

The Walton Family: Boat Builders

With the steamboat trade on the Magnetawan River seriously weakened by the onslaught of trunk roads, by 1912 all three Walton families had settled themselves down in their homes near Wilson Lake on a new waterway—the Pickerel River system. It was to be here just a year later that the Almaguin boat-building family would construct their most famous steamer of all, the *Kawigamog*—the Indian word for "where the waters turn back." Captain Arthur Walton's son Edgar came up with the design for this steamer, and it is little wonder. Since the age of seven, Edgar had worked with his father on the family's steamers that up until now, had been plying the waters of the Magnetawan River. Edgar, besides being a ship designer, also had the distinction of being the youngest man on record at that time, to obtain captain's papers for the operation of passenger steamers on inland waters. He accomplished this feat in 1906 at the age of twenty-six, writing the examinations in St. Catharines, Ontario.[1]

When Captain Arthur Walton made the decision to seek out new business opportunities further north, he made the trip accompanied by his sons Edgar and William. It would take the men three weeks to make the round trip from Magnetawan to Port Loring—on foot. Once back home, Captain Walton informed the family that he had purchased the home and sawmill of Ephreum Ratz and his wife, while son Edgar bought the log home of Robert Brooks.[2] The Ratz family had originally come from Chicago in 1898 and there is some suggestion that Ephreum had a brother by the name of Jacob, whose property was where Port Loring's government dock is situated today. It would be some time later that Edgar purchased the Jacob Ratz property, which contained both a sawmill and gristmill. Later, he would add his own cedar shingle mill to the complex.[3] This property became a fine home for Edgar and his wife, Ellen (Patterson), and children Marjorie, Ethel, Bertha and Enid. Of Edgar's four daughters, Enid would live the longest, passing away in January 1980, at the age of 100.

After arriving in Port Loring, Captain Walton's other son, William, moved in with his father and remained for several months until the Steady home, located half way between Wilson Lake and Loring, was put up for sale. Needless to say the two families had to make do with fairly cramped quarters for those few months, as Arthur and his wife, Rebekah Celesia (Sawyer), were

Four years after Arthur Walton built his first boat, the *Lady Katrine*, the golden era of shipbuilding in Almaguin was underway. Walton's sons, William and Edgar, along with Sam Best, built the *Emulator* in 1890 and the *Glen Rosa* the following year. An unidentified captain and engineer can be seen onboard the *Emulator* pictured here, while four river drivers stand on a log boom alongside the tug. Note the long steel spikes on the boots of the driver, second from right.

looking after their nephew and niece, Ernie and Nellie Sawyer, and son William had his own four children, Aubrey Taylor "Dob," Leith Glenister "Bun," Merrill Linwood "Squirrel" and Daisy Eloise, along with his wife Carolyn "Carrie" Alberta (Taylor).[4]

Timber for the Walton steamboats all came from the Manning lot in Port Loring, east of where Kidd's sawmill would be built in later years. In the early 1970s, this property was bought by Archie Rogerson and became known as Rogerson's Mill. The Walton's flagship the *Kawigamog* would be their largest ship, measuring 72 feet in length and with a gross tonnage of 52 tons. For this endeavour the Walton men were joined by Ernie Sawyer, Arthur's nephew, and construction of the boat began on the shores of Wilson Lake, just south of the former Jacob Ratz mill property. With only limited resources available, they cleverly used what was eventually to be the *Kawigamog*'s boiler to heat up the steam box where the lumber and timbers were primed for a couple of days, to make them pliable enough to be formed into ribs. The bow, it seems, was deliberately built shallow to allow for easier landings for picking up and unloading freight and passengers, since there were no proper docking facilities in the area at that time.[5] To safeguard the vessel, she was outfitted with 3/8 inch steel plating from the bow down past the waterline so she could land almost anywhere without damaging the hull.[6]

The glorious moment came on June 4, 1913, when *Kawigamog* was officially launched. Built sideways to the water, the vessel was poised on the greased skids, ready for the launching lines to be cut. William Walton's wife Carrie was given the honour of christening the steamer with the traditional bottle of champagne. People thronged the site, some of whom had come all the way from Golden Valley to watch the event. The *Kawigamog* drew five feet, six inches of water, and the diameter of her four-bladed propeller was an impressive four feet. According to Dob Walton, she was capable of a speed of ten knots.

With boat traffic waning on the Magnetawan River by 1912, Captain Arthur Walton and his extended family had settled near Wilson Lake on a new waterway—the Pickerel River system. Here the Almaguin family would build their most famous steamer of all, the *Kawigamog*—the Native word for "where the waters turn back." From the years 1913 to 1928, the *Kawigamog* made the seventy-kilometre trip between Duck Lake, south of Port Loring, to Dollars Dam, north of the "S" Narrows, on a regular basis. The photograph is believed to have been taken during the 1923 shipping season.

Taken to the local mill point where she was fitted with her machinery and the main decks, the *Kawigamog* initially ran a few trips from the picnic grounds (later Frank Sweet's tourist camps) to as far as Duck Lake in the summer of 1913. The charge was 25 cents for adults, with children boarding the vessel for free. The trip may have been short but the reality was that the steamer couldn't travel any further—the Pickerel River outlet at Wilson Lake was both too shallow and narrow. When the decision to widen the outlet was made, Captain Arthur Walton operated the steam boiler and compressor for the drills himself, to ensure that the holes for the dynamite were large enough to blast the rocks from the riverbed.[7] Once this was completed, it allowed Wilson Lake to become the home port for the *Kawigamog* and other steamers travelling the Pickerel River. Of course, it also meant that the dam at the lower end of Toad Lake had to be taken out and the bridge at Salines Road had to be built higher to allow the boats to pass. According to Dob Walton, despite the improvements to the bridge, the smokestack on the *Kawigamog* still had to be hinged about eight feet from the top to permit the vessel to pass under this bridge—unless of course the water was low or the fireman simply forgot to lower it! More than once her stack was knocked down by the bridge. Another improvement came in 1915 when the Dollars Dam was raised to a height of about eight feet. It then backed the water up approximately six feet all along the waterway to Duck Lake.[8]

The *Kawigamog*'s maiden voyage to Lost Channel was on May 24, 1915. Dob Walton remembers very clearly the points of interest on this memorable trip. For one thing, there was the beautiful log cabin on the starboard side that belonged to Dr. Beale. What was once known as Beale's Point became Beale's Island, after the water was raised by Dollars Dam. The next cottage was on the port side, belonging to Dr. Jamieson. Just as the steamer passed through the outlet to the Pickerel River, on the starboard side was the Matthew's farm, then Eddie Forsyth's cottage on the port side. Next was Captain Kelsey's cottage named "U Need A Rest."

The *Kawigamog* proceeded through the channel to Toad Lake where the old Wilson Dam had been taken out. Just after passing under the Pickerel Bridge on the port side was the Fleming house and the remains of Blackmoor's mill. Dob remembers vividly how the steamer fairly sailed past The Maples (a summer cottage), through Little Pine Narrows and past the Smokey Creek Dam to the American E.N. Rowell's cottage on the starboard side. Once the *Kawigamog* got through The Elbow and past Blackmoor's new mill on Blackmoor Bay, she landed at Stumpy Bay, located at the extreme end of Lost Channel. According to Dob, the water here had been very shallow until the water was raised by Dollars Dam. Once the passengers disembarked for a shore lunch, those that wanted a little exercise walked over to Cole's Mill on Key Lake. After the tour of the mill everyone sat down to tea and fresh pie. The tea dish, a low bowl without handles, was made out of tin, as were the plates and utensils.[9]

As the steamboat business continued to grow, that same year the Waltons decided to build a warehouse and a dock at Stumpy Bay. A tote road was cut from the warehouse over to Coles Road. The W.H. Cole and Sons Mill used this road to get lumber out to Mowat Station on the CNR. The Waltons would use this route for two years to bring in freight and passengers. Dob Walton remembers that Jim "Pop" Davis was the teamster, while his wife Martha looked after

Once steamship travel was fully operational on the Pickerel River, it opened up a whole new region for the vacationing American sportsman. This postcard shows the summer home of E.N. Rowell, a box manufacturer from Batavia, New York. In the 1880s, Rowell became world famous for his ladies' compact boxes that held dusting powder and face powder. Today, a small selection of surviving Rowell compacts can be found on eBay.

the cooking and housekeeping at the warehouse. Dob himself was barely ten years old when he got his first opportunity to ride out to Mowat Station with Pop. Travelling on this tote road, according to Dob, was some experience. The base of the road was just flat rocks for 100 yards at a time. The ride was anything but smooth.[10]

The second Walton steamer was the *Douglas L.*, built at Port Loring by Edgar Walton for the Schroeder Mills and Timber Company. This was after the company acquired the Lauder, Spears and Howland mill at Lost Channel. James Ludgate named the vessel after his son Douglas, who had died in an accident, the details of which were never disclosed. Up until his death he had been the manager for the lumber company's Key Valley Railway.[11] Besides the *Kawigamog* and the *Douglas L.*, other steamers plying the waters of the Pickerel River included the *Arthur L.*, built by Fred Well and named after its owner, Arthur L. Empey of the Empey Lumber Company. Captained by Robert Cook, the boat's crew consisted of William Brooks, second in command, and Edgar Bowers and Charles Sims as two of the firemen. The Walton nephew, Ernie Sawyer, was the vessel's engineer for a number of years.[12]

Another notable vessel on the Pickerel River was the tugboat, the *Stanley Byers*. It had several owners, among them the Stuart and Donnelly Lumber Company. Captain Walton chartered the

The tugboat *Mike*, owned by the Knight Bros., became a familiar sight on the Magnetawan River, often towing two scows of tanbark at a time. The boat was named after her captain, Mike Pritchard, and said to be the best tug on the river. Most of the boats the Knight Bros. used, like the Mike, transported either logs or tanbark up the river to factories in Burk's Falls. However, by 1934 it had become more economical to ship lumber by rail. That same year the *Mike* became the last tug on the Magnetawan. Its sale marked the end of the steamboat era. Shipped to Meaford by rail, the *Mike* became a Great Lakes fishing boat.

tug for one year to tow lumber, with his nephew Merrill working both as fireman and engineer. While the *Stanley Byers* was the smallest of the tugboats on the Pickerel River, the *Nellie Bly* was described as the strongest boat on the waterways. She had been transported to Lost Channel by flatcar from Toronto and when she was no longer needed, was returned back to the city in the same fashion. Used as a fire tug in Toronto, the vessel was 52 feet long, had a 5 1/2 inch propeller and was powered by a straight high-pressure one-cylinder engine. Locally she was owned by the Schroeder Mills and Timber Company and later by Pakesley Lumber as well as having another local owner on record, the Bruce and Kirk Lumber Company.

Dob Walton remembers that one day as she was towing logs on Duck Lake, the *Nellie Bly* struck a rock and sank. Although the water was over her deck, she was refloated by using two scows, one on either side with timbers across and chains around her hull. Dob explained that in order to raise her, the scows were filled with water and the chains tightened up. When the water was pumped out of the scows, they rose and the *Nellie Bly* came right along with them. She was repaired right at the scene and went on her way.[13] Scows played a large part in the lumber operations along the Pickerel River. Of the ten scows on the river, the Walton family owned three, and the rest were owned by the Schroeder Mills and Timber Company, the Pakesley Lumber Company and the Empey Lumber Company. The majority of these scows were able to carry at least two carloads of lumber that translated into approximately 35,000 running board feet. The two biggest scows, one owned by the Waltons, the other by the Pakesley Lumber Company, could carry three carloads each.[14]

Although Dob Walton was a member of this famous boat-building family, he started in the business quite by accident. Following that memorable trip down the tote road with Pop Davis, it was in June of 1916 when he was ten years old that Dob decided he wanted to spend a few days holidaying on the *Kawigamog*. Dob's brother Bun and cousin Ernest Sawyer were already working as firemen and his other brother Squirrel was the ship's cook. His job consisted of frying potatoes or bacon and sometimes the fish that were caught over the side. There was also the task of making tea and then washing everything up.

One day during that memorable holiday, the fish stuck to the pan, the grease caught on fire and Squirrel threw the whole thing overboard, quitting in disgust. A cook was sorely needed so Dob's father asked him if he'd like the job. He agreed. As the *Kawigamog* was in the process of towing a boom of logs for the Bruce and Kirk Lumber Company, the trip from Duck Lake to Dollars Lake was to take twenty-four days, ending at Dollar's Bridge. For his work as the ship's cook, Dob recalls that he was paid $24, a dollar a day, and it was paid out in one dollar bills. Once back home he immediately ordered a blue serge suit with two pairs of pants, one long pair and one that buckled at the knees, the latter considered all the rage for "young" men of the day. The total cost of the suit was $14 with the remaining money going into the family fund.[15] He was to work a couple of more summers as the ship's cook, but by 1919 at the age of twelve, Dob was promoted to deckhand and was assisting the firemen.

There would be another turning point in Dob's fledgling career in the shipping business. With the Spanish Flu now running rampant in the Loring area, even those on the water weren't safe. Merrill Walton was the first to be stricken on the *Kawigamog* and four days later while on the job, Dob's own father became sick. The steamer was approaching the landing at the Bruce and Kirk Lumber Company's mill when Captain Walton gave the signal to reverse the engines. Too weak to throw the lever over, William Walton collapsed on the deck and the steamer ran into the loading dock. Because the dock was constructed of mainly slab wood and sawdust, the steamer sustained little damage. Dob was advised by his grandfather, Captain Walton, that he would have to take over for his father. The job would last four days until his Uncle Edgar could leave the *Stanley Byers* and take over until Dob's father had recovered.

While Merrill was sick, Maurice Maloney of Sundridge was in charge of firing the engine. During these few days the *Kawigamog* would make a landing at the Schroeder Mills and Timber Company's warehouse, where twenty-two seriously ill lumbermen had been transported by wagons from the company's Camp 2. The hope was that the men could be taken to Lost Channel for treatment as the surrounding lumber camps didn't want the infected in their midst. As Dob remembers, he and Maurice were too young and small to carry the lumbermen on board so they grabbed the sides of the blankets the men were lying on and dragged them on to the deck, side by side. One lumberjack perished before the steamer could make any headway. At the time there were about 2,000 lumberjacks working the camps and mills around Lost Channel and only one doctor, Dr. Clee. There were no facilities at Lost Channel to care for so many desperately sick men, so the men were taken to Schroeder Mills and Timber Company's temporary hospital set back in the woods. The Waltons tended to their own sick with Dob's mother Carrie and his sister Daisy looking after his father and brother. Temporary relief came from cold compresses, using the cold river water.[16]

Over the years, the *Kawigamog* transported a variety of cargo—the only way of getting the goods to the settlers. There would be teams of horses, cattle and camping gear all loaded up together. But the most memorable shipments included twelve tons of honey and then, all that tarpaper! The honey was being shipped by Brunne's Apiary in Arnstein. The apiary stood to save a considerable sum of money on shipping costs, as the twelve tons qualified for the Canadian Pacific Railway carload rate. As for the load of tarpaper, Dob recalled area merchants being persuaded to take the deal by a fast-talking salesman. If every merchant bought 500 rolls each, well then, the salesman wouldn't sell to anyone else. The *Kawigamog* shipped that tarpaper for weeks on end. When there was room after the regular cargo, the hands would simply fill up the space with more tarpaper.[17]

During the summer months, the steamer became an open market. Harky Haggart, who opened the first store in Port Loring, figured that by setting up a stall on the *Kawigamog*, he could sell fresh meat and vegetables to both tourists and the families living in Lost Channel. Haggart's store incidentally, was set up in the former home of Robert Brooks; the last owner had been Edgar Walton. By fall, Haggart would turn to shipping beef quarters to be sold to the Schroeder Mills and Timber Company lumber camps. The meat wasn't wrapped or anything, just stacked on deck like wood. One shipment included 120 quarters. The cattle were slaughtered in the fall and then hung until partially frozen before Haggart would get around to cutting it.[18]

In 1919, Harky Haggart ventured into a new enterprise, opening a hotel on Wilson Lake. He named it the Lakeview Hotel, but it appears he wasn't cut out for the business, as he sold it only ten years later to Oscar Clapperton. He added eight new cottages and ran the hotel until 1946. Renamed Simp's Landing, it closed down in 2004, under the ownership of Ron and Pat Simpson.[19]

With business booming for the Waltons in 1923, at the age of sixteen Dob was made purser on the *Kawigamog* and that year made 208 return trips to Lost Channel, sometimes making as many as three trips in one day.[20] Although the *Kawigamog* was not the only steamer to tow log booms to bush mills and railway sidings, she was the most famous. From the years 1913 to 1928, the steamer made the seventy-kilometre trip between Duck Lake south of Port Loring to Dollars Dam, north of the "S" Narrows, on a regular basis.

In later years gas-powered boats joined the steamers on Pickerel River, including the *Adanac* owned by Captain Tulley of Loring. It was operated for a time by Ted Manning and

Sport fishing was so successful in the Loring area that it became a popular feature for novelty postcards. Here is a vintage scene from Loring and nearby Deer Lake, showing a range of fish from smallmouth black bass to speckled trout. With no catch limits or slot sizes in place in those days, fishermen caught as many as could be cleaned in one day.

Ray Thompson. Another gas-powered boat was the *Clapperton*, later purchased by the Waltons and renamed *Daisy*, after William's daughter. Most of these boats were about thirty feet in length and used for transporting both passengers and light freight. When in 1922 work began on improving the rugged, wagon trail from Trout Creek to Loring, the Pickerel River was already beginning to lose its importance as a transportation corridor. A few cars and trucks starting appearing and it was indeed an event when the first driver ventured out from Trout Creek, arriving in Loring five hours later.[21] By the time the road improvements were completed in 1924, the timber stands were just about played out and the large mills at places like Lost Channel shut down. Smaller mills were dismantled and shipped to other locations. At the end, the *Kawigamog*, like many of the steamers of her era, was deliberately scuttled off the dock at Port Loring into a watery grave. Dob Walton acknowledged that the *Kawigamog* was getting old and there was little left for her to do.[22]

But what had made the *Kawigamog* so well suited to her job, remembers Dob, is the fact she was the only steamer with ice-breaking capabilities. Her ice-breaking equipment was handmade and capable of breaking up to three inches of solid ice. "And there wasn't ever a hunting season," said Dob, "that went by without the steamer encountering ice. There would be times that the ice was so thick the hunters would walk out to the steamer and either hand the deckhands their mail, retrieve incoming mail, or collect provisions. And more times than naught, there would be only a path through the ice formation on the river that went on for miles and just wide enough to get the *Kawigamog* through." He recalled that on one occasion after the *Kawigamog* had left Port Loring at eight o'clock in the morning and had picked up a couple of hunters along the route, the temperature was dropping so fast that by the time the steamer reached The Maples, the ice was so thick she had to back up and ram it a couple of times. There were also times when the *Stanley Byers* joined in and pushed the *Kawigamog* through the ice, while the hunters just slept on deck or on the woodpile, wherever there was room.[23]

Captain Arthur Walton was the eldest of the steamboat captains on the Pickerel River and he captained the *Kawigamog* for almost its entire life. He died on October 19, 1929, at the age of eighty-three, and had operated the boat up until nine days before his death. As his grandson Dob phrased it in his interview with *Almaguin News*, one could say that the captain died with his boots on. Following his death, Dob's father William took over the Port Loring operation, including the family's flagship, the *Kawigamog*. Although a Captain Drew from Parry Sound had come to Port Loring to captain the Walton's steamboat, he was more accustomed to the Great Lakes freighters. On the day he left Dob recalls Captain Drew retorting, "He wouldn't run a steamboat in the bush." With the end of the season nearing, Dob was left to captain the *Kawigamog* for the remaining months. The next year William Walton had Captain Tom Kennedy of Burk's Falls take over the job for the next couple of years.[24]

The shipping season for the *Kawigamog* usually started the first week of May, but Dob Walton remembers the earliest run the vessel ever made was on April 24. Although he didn't remember the year, she was nearing the end of her life. On that day, the Pickerel River was almost blocked with logs that had been dumped on the ice during the winter months and had now formed booms. The *Kawigamog* picked her way through the booms, remembers Dob, with the deckhands poling over the boom chains. On the return trip eleven booms were counted, now all tied off so that there would be a channel for the steamer to pass through. Dob estimates there were about 100,000 logs in the river that spring.[25]

William Walton obtained his marine engineer papers at the age of twenty-one and was described by his family as a good sort of person. "Never drank," said his son Dob, "seldom smoked and the closest he got to swearing was the occasional 'dammit.'" During the annual marine inspection at Lost Channel, officials would often comment that Walton always kept the *Kawigamog*'s machinery in top condition. Of all the engineers on the Pickerel River, Walton was deemed the most experienced and he was the *Kawigamog*'s engineer for almost her entire life. Blessed with an exceptionally good memory over the years, William Walton came to remember the names of the majority of passengers travelling on the steamer.

"The *Kawigamog* had provided us with a way of life for a number of years and more importantly, had played a major role in opening up the Loring area to lumbering and tourism. Perhaps the story of the *Kawigamog* can be summed up by quoting a little verse that Dixie Wilson wrote in my sister Daisy's autograph book," said Dob:

Some friends are entertaining
Some are even boring
But the best friends I ever had
Resided in Port Loring.
And when my days are over
And I hand in my final log
I want to think of my happiest days
Spent on the *Kawigamog*.[26]

A Life Remembered: Richard Thomas (1932–2006)

Some believed him to be a bit unorthodox, while others lauded him as a man of great independence in both thought and action. According to his widow, however, no one knew the real Richard Thomas. "Even his sister, Jean Comfort, didn't really know him. Whenever people talked about Richard they spoke of him in relation to themselves," said a sorrowful Jenny Thomas, adding, "He was *my* life and he was taken away from *me*. He used to say he wasn't as fast on his feet as I was. I think we were a good match—a good pair." But whatever people's perception of him was, and how just by being acquainted with him they felt it made a difference in their lives, for Richard Thomas, the man, it was a life well-lived. Over the years his many talents would see him through a variety of careers, from a youthful footloose adventurer, to a radio and television personality, environmentalist, family man, writer and last but not least, a politician.

Richard Thomas was seriously injured in a single vehicle accident on the morning of December 27, 2005, on Highway #11 at the north entrance to Burk's Falls. When he succumbed to his injuries on February 22, 2006, he held the seat of Reeve of Armour Township in southeast Parry Sound District. Although at the time, running for office had been the furthest thing from his mind, the 2003 municipal elections would find him elected to the head of the municipal council with a comfortable majority. What prompted Richard to throw his hat in the ring was the fact that even though it had been three years earlier, the discord emanating from the 2000 local election had yet to die down. Allegations of voting irregularities had thrust the municipality in to a long and dragged-out court case that divided not only council but the community. Richard Thomas wanted the dissension put to an end, and he poured himself into the task. Many will say that's the type of man he was. Although his political career would span more than a quarter of a century, beginning and ending with municipal affairs, there was to be a lot more in between.

Richard Malcolm Thomas was born in downtown Toronto on February 4, 1932, the youngest of nine children. He never talked much about his childhood, but it is little wonder. His father, Welshman Herbert Edgar Thomas, left his mother Gladys Gertrude (Brook) and the family shortly after Richard's birth. The young Richard attended Huron Street Public School

Sir Richard Thomas, Mendelson Joe, artist, 2001. "The voice (or pen) of sanity as delivered in his columns for the *Almaguin News*."

and later Jarvis Collegiate, but dropped out after Grade 10 and hit the road. With no clear destination in mind, he got as far as Barrie where the suave teenager with the golden voice landed his first radio job—with CKBB. However, his itchy feet got the better of him and a few years later he was on the road again, this time heading to the west coast. At the same time there was someone else en route to the coast—Jane Anne "Jenny" Campbell—Richard's future wife. Their paths would ultimately cross at a Vancouver radio station.

Having grown up in Moose Jaw, Saskatchewan, Jenny explained that, in those days, everyone headed for Vancouver because it was the thing to do. "So I went. Today, the destination is more like Hawaii." She recalled that shortly after she landed a job as the receptionist at CJOR, Richard Thomas walked through the door. "Before I could look up to see who it was, I heard his voice. Little did I realize I would continue to hear that voice for the next fifty-three years." Richard had come to the office quite by chance, and decided he wanted to speak to the station manager—without an appointment. Jenny didn't think he'd be successful, but the young man, bursting with confidence knocked on the door and was immediately invited inside. Later as he was leaving, Jenny asked how it went. Richard Thomas informed her that she was now looking at CJOR's newest radio personality. She laughed, "He was the new night guy, who then asked me out for coffee." Of course, the invitation came with a condition—she'd have to buy her own coffee. Jenny agreed. It turned out Richard had hitchhiked up the west coast to British Columbia with only the clothes on his back and very little money in his pocket. He certainly didn't have enough to pay for two coffees.

The couple eventually were married in Edmonton in 1953—while Richard was working for CFRN—one in a string of radio stations where he would be employed over the next twenty years. Over and over again it would be Richard's golden voice and his savvy on knowing how to use it that wowed both radio executives and the audiences. On the other hand, his open contempt for those he viewed as not caring enough for Planet Earth and his refusal to toe the corporate line, gained him notoriety with management and advertisers alike. Working his way through the radio hierarchy as announcer, writer, producer and programmer, he would gain the most recognition for his innovations, which became the standard bearers in Canadian broadcasting, particularly when it came to the country's first FM stations including Toronto's CHFI-FM in the late 1950s and CHUM-FM in the 1960s. Richard also set forth a new vision for CBC radio, but by 1966, he'd had enough and for a time put radio on the back burner.

He moved his family out of Toronto to the Town of Kearney in the Parry Sound District, located just on the fringe of the western boundary of Algonquin Park. Here he built a home of logs reclaimed from an old barn and set up a recording studio. That studio became a mecca for musicians from around the world as well as a place for Richard to produce his own unique brand of radio programs that became increasingly popular with European audiences. At the same time he began producing tapes, every sound bite resonating with his rich voice. Said his wife Jenny, "Richard loved to do tapes, and did lots of them. And then he'd give them all away."

During his first meeting with the young editor of the *Almaguin News* in 1976, Richard advised Allan Dennis, that he considered himself a maverick, "After being fired from eighteen

Pictured here outside the Burk's Falls Courthouse in his converted Volvo, the defiant Richard Thomas eventually saw the charges of bootlegging that had been brought against him dropped. The RCMP had originally accused Thomas in December of 1980 of "producing spirits without a licence" and seized his still.

of twenty-three radio stations because I disagreed with the manner and quality of the shows being aired, you can see for yourself the reason for the label 'maverick.'" Although Richard left radio, it never really left him. For a number of years afterwards he earned the bulk of his income from radio and television commercials. The list was impressive: Molson, Gulf Oil, Kraft Foods—Canada's "Ben" promoting Cracker Barrel Cheese, to name just a few. At the height of his career he was considered one of the top three talents in the field in Canada. But there were more pressing things for him to do now… like making moonshine. No, not bootleg whisky, but ethyl alcohol. Make no mistake Richard Thomas was no illegal distiller.

In the late 1970s, Richard decided it was time to step up to the plate and do something in a personal way to address modern society's overdependence on crude oil. His homemade still was churning out ethyl alcohol at a frightening pace, all produced from Jerusalem artichokes grown on his own land. Converting his 1970 Volvo from gasoline to alcohol, Richard estimated that his one-and-one-third acre of artichokes had yielded approximately 300 gallons of fuel for his vehicle, at about 30 cents a gallon. He was eager to draw attention to his experiment, and he soon got it—from the law. He made newspaper headlines in December 1980, when the RCMP seized his still and charged him under the Excise Act for producing spirits without a licence. The charges were eventually withdrawn, and shortly afterwards Richard was invited by the United Nations Institute of Training and Research to prepare a course on integrated food and fuel agriculture for developing countries. "The Government of Canada recognized the need for the development of energy alternatives, including the possibility of alcohol fuels produced on a small scale," wrote Ontario's Deputy-Attorney General, H. Allan Leal, Q.C., announcing the reasons for the decision.

But just shortly before Richard Thomas acquired all that notoriety for running a still, he became involved in municipal politics as a Perry Township councillor. Then, in 1981, following his success in promoting the alternative fuel source, Richard decided to leave local politics and run as a Liberal candidate for the provincial riding of Parry Sound. It was his first try at provincial politics and many of his supporters were excited about the possibility of sending someone to Queen's Park who could think outside the box. Interestingly enough, campaign advertisements of the time didn't even acknowledge that Richard was running for the Liberals. One local advertisement read, "Democracy is giving Parry Sound Riding a chance to send a brilliant man to Queen's Park. Richard Thomas will be the most exciting man in Parliament. And he will be representing us. ELECT THOMAS. Sponsored by the East Parry Sound Committee to Elect Richard Thomas." And Parry Sound riding almost did.

Richard narrowly lost to the man who would eventually become the Conservative Premier of Ontario, Ernie Eves. A judicial recount of the March 19 election gave Eves 8,995 votes to Thomas's 8,989, a difference of only six votes. The election results earned Eves the nickname of "Landside Ernie," while the experience only whetted Richard Thomas' appetite for politics. His next step up the political ladder was his bid for the leadership of the Ontario Liberal Party. Just a year later at the February 21, 1982, Liberal convention, Thomas placed third, garnering 11 percent of the vote, behind David Peterson (who eventually won) and Sheila Copps. Copps, for

This Time — Let's Do Better!

Meet **Richard Thomas**

Your Liberal Candidate in Parry Sound Riding

Don't miss your opportunity to vote! If you cannot vote on **March** 19 please use the advance polls. Advance poll dates are Saturday, March 14, and Monday, March 16.

Be sure your name is on the voters' list . . . you are eligible to vote if:
- you have attained eighteen years of age
- you are a Canadian citizen or other British subject
- you have resided in Ontario for the twelve months next preceding the day of polling
- you reside in the electoral district
- you are not disqualified under the Election Act or otherwise prohibited by law from voting.

I believe All Candidates Meetings give voters their best chance to size up their candidates, don't you? Please try to organize one in your neighbourhood.

To get to know me better please turn the page.

Thank you.

"This Time—Let's Do Better!" In 1981, Richard Thomas decided to run for the Ontario Liberal Party as a candidate in the District of Parry Sound. Richard narrowly lost to the man who would eventually become the Conservative premier of Ontario, Ernie Eves—by six votes.

those who may have forgotten was the first Liberal in over fifty years to represent the provincial riding of Hamilton Centre, and under Prime Minister Jean Chrétien she became Canada's first female Deputy Prime Minister. Thomas's bid for the leadership could be considered a success—driven in his desire to spread the message of energy alternatives—in spite of his lack of experience in party politics and lack of a seat in the legislature. But, it almost ruined him financially.

At the time, the *Almaguin News* reported that following the leadership convention, Richard Thomas had spent more than $40,000 of his own money and, along with his wife, was now faced with a whole new slate of challenges. The couple moved from Kearney to Emsdale and a few years later, to a farm in Armour Township just north of Burk's Falls, where Jenny Thomas continues to reside here to this day.

Richard would run one more time against Ernie Eves, but by this time the Big Blue Machine was ready for him. The 1985 election results were nowhere near what they were the first time the two candidates faced each other at the polls. It was around this time that Thomas once again caught the attention of the *News* editor, Allan Dennis. Covering a meeting of the Muskoka-Nipissing-Parry Sound Cattlemen's Association, Dennis observed Thomas, and while listening to his presentation thought, "I should get Richard to write a column for us." Thomas took to the idea like a duck to water. The rest as they say is history. For the next eighteen years readers were greeted by Richard Thomas' weekly commentary beginning with "Ask a Dumb Question." The premise was that more dumb questions needed to be asked in the world. "Dumb questions poke into things that seem so obvious we should be embarrassed to ask about them. Sometimes though, they find a thin spot in what we thought was true and let new light shine in on things we had forgotten. The kind of question that strips away the emperor's clothes," is how Thomas introduced his new column in 1985.

Five years later, in 1990, Richard Thomas would take one last stab at provincial politics. Forming the local chapter of the Green Party and running as its candidate in the election, he garnered 17 percent of the votes, the best the party had ever done in Ontario. He would continue to support the Green Party right up until 2001.

Richard's passion for politics and writing equalled his passion for water. "We've always tried to live by the water," said Jenny Thomas. In fact, both Richard and Jenny were lifeguards at one point in their lives. "When we were in Toronto, we lived at Neville Park in the city's east end, at the end of the Queen streetcar line. It is where our daughters Nell and Sarah were born," she added. By then the couple already had two children, their first born, daughter Pandora, and a son Jeremy. There will be those old timers at CHFI-FM who will remember Richard's days at Neville Park. While most people in the city took public transit or drove to work, Richard would occasionally show up at the office with his canoe. To get to the job on time he would canoe from home along the shoreline of Lake Ontario to the foot of Yonge Street and then portage his way through the downtown core to the studio. Jenny laughs when she recalls those days. "He was a big, strong guy who could portage the canoe anywhere." Richard himself enjoyed telling tales of his stint as a young radio personality in Toronto, canoeing into work, thinking up a story with every stroke. Although Richard enjoyed recreational water activities like canoeing, when it came to swimming, there was nothing else like it for him. He despised the winter because it kept him out of the water longer than he cared. Right through to the last summer of his life, as long as the temperatures allowed it, he took his daily swim.

Taking a moment to reflect on her husband's final days, Jenny said, "When Richard was in hospital, I went down to Neville Park to take a look at where we had once lived. The sky was steely, the water was steely and the waterworks property, well, it was all barricaded off. I couldn't see the building."

Richard Thomas died of his injuries on February 22, 2006, at St. Michael's Hospital in Toronto. In keeping with his wishes, there was no funeral. On April 8, 2006, a memorial celebrating his life was held at the Burk's Falls, Armour, Ryerson Arena. Over 300 people attended the tribute and many were to share their memories of this great man. Some were thought provoking, others downright funny. And yes, some of the anecdotes had to do with water follies! The mourners would take delight in a true story from around 1970 when the Thomases first arrived in Kearney: One particular day found Richard parking his Cadillac convertible outside the Kearney General Store. He stepped inside the shop, the next thing Richard knew, someone was stealing his Caddy. It seems that a young teenage hitchhiker, who had just arrived in town, took the vehicle and drove it straight into the lake. Richard's response? "It probably needed a wash anyways." Even more amazing than his comment was the fact that Richard took the fellow aside and put $300 in his hand before going about his business.

He was never shy about speaking his mind, yet one question remains. After living such a full life, did Richard have any regrets? "Yes," says his widow. "He felt though at the end of his life, he didn't get a chance to be a lawyer, get a degree. It really nagged at him." As for holding the service for her husband at the arena hall, said Jenny, "Richard was a real fan of the arena in Burk's Falls. That's why we [the Thomas family] decided to hold his memorial here. I think we set a precedent," said Jenny. "I think he would have approved."[1]

A Boy Scout's Journey and Lake Cecebe's Green Bay

It's not every day one runs into a career Boy Scout, but that's what makes the 1st Burk's Falls Scout troop so unique. Elwood Addison, a.k.a. Scouter Addie, was the troop's scoutmaster for almost twenty years, having taken on the role in September of 1958. It was supposed to be a temporary position, but lasted until August of 1978. As he would explain, he remained as scoutmaster because there was no one else. Elwood Addison was a Boy Scout first and foremost and over time would also assume the roles of Venturer leader in 1975–76, as well as Rover leader. "I took on these other two positions because again, they could not find a leader. And also, so that these senior boys could carry on the Scouting movement," he added.

Looking back on the many years he has spent with the Scouts, the retired schoolteacher recently quipped, "I've been around so long I'm now the Troop mascot!" In 1965, Elwood was presented with a Long Service medal by District Commissioner Ray Smith, and in 1967, a Medal of Merit for good service to Scouting. Then, in 2003, Elwood was recognized by Scouts Canada Shining Waters Region for his many years of volunteer service to the Scouting movement. More accolades were to follow over the next few years.

The history of the Burk's Falls Boy Scouts is as interesting as the people who were, and still are involved in the local youth organization. In 2007, the local Scouting movement celebrated its 75th anniversary alongside the 100th anniversary of Scouts Canada. From the very beginning, Burk's Falls Lions Club has been the Scouting group's sole sponsor. Although the Lions Club was formed in 1938, a few years after the fledgling troop began holding meetings, Lions members took on the sponsorship with great enthusiasm. That enthusiasm continues to this very day, with the Club providing funds towards programming, building projects at Green Bay Scout Camp—as well as providing funding for the annual Scout Jamboree—if local Scouts were planning to attend.

It was during the early 1930s that Bill Ware, the Baptist minister's son, became the first Lone Scout. One could say he founded the local troop. The very first meetings were held in the loft of the shed behind the McKenzie Street home of Dr. A.W. Partridge. In 1935, when Ernie Warner (1884–1957), the publisher/editor of the *Burk's Falls Arrow*, later the *Almaguin News*

In 1935 when Ernie Warner, the publisher/editor of the *Burk's Falls Arrow*, became the first scoutmaster, there were fifteen Scouts and twelve Cubs. The weekly meetings were switched to the *Arrow* office beside St. Andrew's Presbyterian Church. Pictured here are just a few of the Scouts from that year. Front row: Bill Cripps (left), Cliff Cripps (second from right) and Peter Hunter (right); back row: John Fell (second from left) and Harvey Stewart (third from left). The others are not identified.

(Almaguin Publishing (1989) Limited), became the first scoutmaster, there were fifteen Scouts and twelve Cubs. At this time the weekly meetings were switched to the *Arrow* office.

Key to the success of any Scouting movement is the Scout camp. As Elwood explains, "Here was an opportunity for the boys to play, work and plan and live together under different circumstances than home." What is known of the first Scout camp comes from the recollections of old timers Ted Bunt and Myron Moore. According to them the camp was held at Port Carmen. After that, the next two camps were on Lake Bernard. The first one was on a beach that is now part of Lake Bernard Park, the second on the beach that eventually became known as the Pipes O' Pan. By this time Elwood Addison was old enough to join Cubs. He recalls with some enthusiasm, heading out for the ten-day camp on the back of a truck. "I remember going out in Vic McIndoo's and Art Thompson's vehicles. The cost for camp was 50 cents and a basket of vegetables." Scoutmaster Ernie Warner, or "Boss" as he was fondly called, had Scout members who were Rover age, so they were called upon time to time, to assist him at the summer camps. Elwood's father Edwin also helped out, as did Eldon Booth. Pots, pans and

Before temporarily disbanding because of the Second World War, the Burk's Falls Boy Scouts met at Joseph Hilliar's garage. Front row (l–r): Doug Culbert, Roddy Hunter, Murray Bradford, Sam Goulding, Dave Wittick, Al Gibson and Jim Webber; back row (l–r): Elwood Addison, Milt Wittick, Jack Wilson, Edwin "Buck" Addison, Don Graham, Jack Metcalf, John Metcalf, Ron Culbert and Billy Phillips.

dishes were "washed" in the beach sand and rinsed off in the lake. The boys would then lay them out to dry on the rocks. Refrigeration was a stone crib hole in the ground. According to Elwood, in those days there were no such things as sleeping bags or air mattresses, so everyone made their own "flea bag." The first thing each Scout did was collect four poles to build a frame the size of a single bed. Once the frame was built, a layer of balsam boughs was fitted in to get a springy effect. Over this went a pile of ferns. The "flea bag" was a sheet folded in half, with upwards of three blankets folded and fitted into each other and held in place at the bottom and one side with blanket pins. Each morning the bag would be taken apart to air, and reassembled a few hours later.

When the Depression hit, money was very scarce in rural areas and the holiday season could be bleak for many families. So, to brighten the Christmas morning, damaged toys were collected, carefully repaired and painted by the Boy Scouts of Burk's Falls before being distributed to the needy families—just like Santa Claus. However, when war was declared in 1939, membership took a drop as most of the older Scouts headed to the recruiting offices to sign up. Elwood Addison was just barely into his teens, so he moved on to Scouts.

In 1941, the troop was holding its meetings in Joseph Hilliar's garage before moving to the Orange Hall behind the Baptist church. However, because of declining enrollment, it was decided to temporarily disband Scouting until the fall of 1944. It was then that Frank Partridge, the son of Dr. A.W. Partridge, took over as the Lone scoutmaster, with Elwood Addison being given a passing grade on his Tenderfoot test. When the Japanese surrendered on August 14, 1945, Elwood remembers Art Thompson coming out to the camp on Lake Bernard and busing the Scouts back to Burk's Falls. Here, the troop witnessed the burning of an effigy of Tojo in front of the post office. "We went back to camp later," remembers Elwood. During the Second World War, Hideki Tojo was a Japanese army general and later the country's prime minister, who eventually was hanged as a war criminal.

It would be a year later in November of 1946 that "Skipper," as Frank Partridge was fondly called, along with Jack Wilson, Milt Wittick, George Radford and Elwood Addison, headed to a place called Green Bay on Lake Cecebe. Unbeknownst to them at the time, they were making history by clearing the way for a permanent Scout camp for the local youth. The following year Skipper managed to convince his father to donate his entire forty-seven-acre property with its mile-long shoreline to the Burk's Falls Boy Scouts. The 1947 summer camp was deemed an overwhelming success.

With the troop working hard at fundraising, and being totally supported by the community, they were able to purchase a 16-foot cedar-strip boat, measuring 55 inches wide. Elwood would write in his log that the new Scout boat made its first trip to Green Bay on June 29, 1947. The Agar family of Burk's Falls who summered on Lake Cecebe kindly offered the use of their landing and their boathouse as a supply base for the Scouts. The Scout boat would be used extensively that first summer, making regular supply runs as well as being used for pleasure trips. Popular places visited by the Troop members included the Village of Magnetawan, Pine Point, Twin Islands and Echo Rock.

Elwood remembers that five boys and their leader Alf Harden from Sprucedale joined the Burk's Falls Scouts that first summer. "This small group came part way into camp on the Magnetawan side by jeep and then hiked in," he explained. But to ensure everything was ready, on August 10, a day before the official opening of the camp, the Scouts used the boat to tow a wood cookstove to Green Bay. The stove was carefully secured to a raft made by the young Scouts. Once the boat reached shore and the stove hauled up to the camp kitchen, the raft was used for swimming. As for the camp kitchen, it was set up on four posts, and at mealtimes the Scouts would line up get their food and then sit outside to eat it. "If it was raining, you would run to your tent with your food," explained Elwood. "We always had grace before meals. At first, only the leader would say it but by the end of camp each one would have put his hand up to say grace. Some boys, who were not accustomed to the practice, would learn one grace at camp."

With membership predominantly of the Christian denomination, the Burk's Falls Scout movement continues to place an emphasis on religion, particularly at camp. "We always had a Scouts' Own Service on Sunday," said Elwood. "Some of the boys would take part in the

Under the leadership of Alf Harden, Boys Scouts from Sprucedale attended the first Green Bay Scout Camp in the summer of 1947. Pictured here in the front row (l–r) are Stewart Cowie and Gib Metcalf; in the back row (l–r) are George Chaplin, Arnold Metcalf and Bill Pearce.

service and the Scouter in charge or the district commissioner would take the devotional talk. Sometimes a local minister would be invited to come to deliver the sermon. The service would last about thirty minutes, but it was a quiet time for the boys to enjoy God's Cathedral." In 1958, Elwood Addison built a stone altar or pulpit at Cedar Point and to this day when a Scout camp is in session, a Scout's Own Service is held on the Sunday, out at this special place of worship.

Skipper once asked the question, "Why be a Boy Scout?" His answer would be found in Lord Baden-Powell's *Scouting for Boys*. In his Scouting primers, Baden-Powell included a quote by U.S. President Franklin Delano Roosevelt, one he made during an inspection of Boy Scouts in London, England. In turn, Skipper also included the quotation in one of the troop's 1947 monthly newsletters, *The Etc. & Also.* The president said, "I believe in outdoor games and I do not mind in the least that they are rough games, or that those who take part in them are occasionally injured. I have no sympathy with the overwrought sentiment which would keep a young man in cotton wool. The out-of-doors man must always prove the better in life's contest. When you play, play hard, and when you work, work hard. But do not let your play and your sport interfere with your study."

Frank Partridge was the most beloved scoutmaster of the 1st Burk's Falls Scouts. He is pictured here at the first Scout camp held at Green Bay on Lake Cecebe in August of 1947. That same year Skipper's father, Dr. A. W. Partridge, donated his entire 47-acre waterfront property to the local troop.

For Frank Partridge, the president's message was clear. Skipper would often remark, "Boys should be trained to manliness and not allowed to drift into poor-spirited wasters who can only look on at men's work." He advised members of the 1st Burk's Falls Scouts that one of the chief aims of Scouting is to train youth to look after themselves, so that the youth would "Be Prepared" when the time came for them to take their place as a man. For Elwood Addison, he admits that as a young lad, he ran into temptations the same as other boys. "I am thankful to my scoutmaster Frank Partridge, for steering me away from these problems, as they could have turned out serious for me." In later years when he became Scoutmaster "Addie," he was able "to do the same" as he put it, for certain boys.

The year 1949 started off on a high note for the local Scout troop. On February 18 during a Burk's Falls Lions Club banquet, presentations were made to Patrol Leaders Murray McKay, Edwin Addison, Sam Goulding and Everett Doherty, awarding them their 1st Class badges. Milton Wittick joined Elwood Addison as an assistant scoutmaster to Skipper. Then, less than three months later, the unthinkable would happen. As Elwood Addison would write in his Scout log, "May 2, was the most tragic day in our Scout history. Our scoutmaster Frank Partridge (Skipper) was killed when he was struck by a mallet when another man was driving in a post. Next day, we put the Scout flag at half mast. May 4, at our meeting, I read a scripture, 'Boss' Warner lead in prayer, then 24 of us filed past his casket."

The obituary ran in the May 11, 1949. edition of the *Burk's Falls Arrow*, it read:

> Franklin Henry Partridge—Probably one of the largest funerals ever to be held in Burk's Falls was witnessed last Thursday, when Frank Partridge was laid to rest after dying from the cause of an accident as reported last week.
>
> The United Church was filled to capacity. The Boy Scouts and Girl Guides formed a Guard of honour both at the church and the cemetery. Rev. E. Moorhouse gave a brief address of sympathy and encouragement.

In 1949, May 2 would be one of the darkest days in history for the Burk's Falls Scouts. Scoutmaster Frank Partridge succumbed to his injuries following a farming accident. His funeral a few days later was one of the largest ever to be held in Burk's Falls, with the local United Church filled to capacity. Pictured here, the Boy Scouts and Girl Guides form an honour guard as Skipper's casket leaves the church.

The pallbearers were Messers. Stan Darling, Don Graham (Huntsville), Billie Cripps, Alan Armstrong, John Fell, and Ken Varcoe.

The floral tributes were extremely beautiful and there were about 50 pieces presented.

Frank was a native of Burk's Falls, having been born twenty-five years ago. He received his education locally and when World War II broke out he joined the Canadian Navy and became an instructor at the York depot at Toronto. On returning home he took a great interest in all municipal welfare work. He became a member of the Village Council, Scout Master of the local Troop which he built up to efficiency. He was 2nd vice president of the Lions Club, a member of the Rink committee and took a keen interest in every phase of Agriculture, organizing the Boy's Potato Club and other activities. There was not a good work in town that Frank was not interested in. His passing has left an immense blank in the community.

He married in May of 1946 to Jean McLachlan of Magnetawan who with an infant daughter, Julia Anne survives. Also surviving are his parents. Dr. A.W. and Mrs. Partridge and four sisters,—Margaret (Mrs. Frank Mitchell), Ruth (Mrs. Frank Wesley), Beatrice (Mrs. Stan McVey), and Mary (Mrs. J. Emerson).

The day the newspaper came out, the Burk's Falls Scouts held a group committee meeting where "Mickey" McNaughton was appointed the next scoutmaster, with Milton Wittick and Elwood Addison in turn, conducting the Scout meeting as assistant scoutmasters. Although deeply saddened by what had happened, Scouting continued, with Milton and Elwood meeting with the new scoutmaster on July 7 to plan the summer camp. It was a quiet start to the summer of 1949, with the only activity being an overnight hike in July taken by troop members Gordon Brear and Clayton Young. Elwood would write in his log that on August 2, he and Milton went to Green Bay to pitch the HQ tent, with the boys following the next day. There were sixteen Scouts attending camp that year and immediately after the tents were pitched—it began to pour rain. Opening day also saw Mr. LaBarre's American Scouts stopping at Green Bay on their canoe trip through Lake Cecebe along the Magnetawan River system.

With the camp in full swing by the second day, the KP (Kitchen Patrol) would be up by seven o'clock to start breakfast, remembered Elwood. "There would be no sleeping in," he added. "One patrol would be in charge of the meals and cleanup for a day, then change when another patrol took its turn." When it came to the Scouts' favourite pastime—swimming—regulations were strict. There were two options, the ring system, and the buddy system. "The Scout put his ring up on a board opposite his name when he went in the water and took it off if he left the swimming area," explained Elwood. "When the person in charge noticed that there were six rings up and only five heads, then the boys would be called out of the water to double check. If one boy had gone to his tent and forgot to take his ring off the board, then he would lose a swim period. No excuses."

Summer camp at Green Bay would often see individual patrols and sometimes the whole troop leave the permanent camp for an overnight hike, which meant no tents. For a number of Scouts, an overnight would be the first time he had ever slept out under the stars. As for the last night of camp, well, according to Elwood, that's when the Scouts could get into all sorts of hijinks. "In 1949 when Milton and I were the assistant scoutmasters, we heard that the boys were going to get us! The two of us rolled up our 'sleeping bags' and went back in the bush behind Cedar Point. The boys tramped the bush until they found us, and then threw a bucket of water on each of us! They sure took off fast. My bed was okay but Milt's was soaked so we returned to camp." But as the assistant scoutmasters discovered, the only person left at camp was Scoutmaster Mickey McNaughton. "Everyone had taken off back to the field for the rest of the night, in case of retaliation," said Elwood. There was no harm done, but as Scout leaders, it was made sure that this type of activity was kept to a minimum.

It was to be almost ten years later that the Scouting Group Committee, comprised of Harvey Fowler and Ted Bunt, to name a few, approached Elwood to see if he would consider becoming the scoutmaster. "I thought it would be a wonderful challenge, until I began to realize the awesome responsibility. I told them to try and find someone else and I would continue as the assistant." Insisting that the position would be "temporary" until the committee could round up someone else, Elwood took the bait. "Now that is history because I held that position for the next nineteen years!"

After marrying his high school sweetheart, Bonnie Walker, in 1954, Elwood quickly recruited her and she became a valuable "assistant" to the troop. She was often called upon to transport the boys to and from camp and also accompanied the troop on trips. Bonnie was certainly up to the task, as she helped out on Apple Day, took the snowmobile out on occasion to Green Bay to bring the boys back from camp, and went for the doctor, and so on. Said Elwood, "I had to work and got only a little time off for these extra activities." To her credit, Bonnie Addison picked up the slack.

Although Scouter Addie left the 1st Burk's Falls Scouts in 1978 to take a teaching position at a high school in southern Ontario, following his retirement in 1994, he received a request from the then Scoutmaster Doug Brown "Samwyz," to rejoin the troop. With Elwood having guided Doug Brown through Scouts, Venturers and ultimately as a Rover, he consented, but only if he could come back as a counsellor. It's a position he's held to this day. And, after more than fifty years of marriage to a Boy Scout, Bonnie Addison remains at his side. Every time there's a new member needing uniform accessories, she'll whip out her sewing machine and begin making the distinctive blue and red trimmed neckerchief, proudly sporting the Lions international crest.

One of the most important events to take place at Green Bay Scout Camp was during the August Civic Holiday weekend of 2001, when a cairn was dedicated to Scoutmaster Frank Partridge. With Elwood taking charge of the project's fundraising campaign, the construction of the memorial became a labour of love for a former Scout, Rick Dingman of Magnetawan. Over the summer months, Dingman would transport over thirty bags of cement across the lake to the camp and then begin tirelessly collecting rock together. When completed, the cairn was positioned to overlook Green Bay itself. The inscription on top reads:

> This property (47 A) was donated by Dr. A. W. Partridge in 1947. The cairn is erected in memory of his son, Scoutmaster Frank Partridge (Skipper), 1924–1949; he was a devoted and respected Scouter.

Family members in attendance for the dedication ceremony were Frank's daughter Julie of Toronto, and his surviving sisters, Mary of Arizona and Beatrice of Parry Sound. "My father died when I was young. I have discovered that he was not only a father figure, but mentor, always urging people to strive for more than they thought they could do," is how Julie would begin her speech of thanks to the crowd. As she would point out, her trip to Green Bay Scout Camp would mark a milestone in her journey to find out more about her late father. For Frank's sisters, the occasion was almost too overwhelming. So many people had come together to celebrate the life of their father and brother. Mary and Beatrice let it be known that the doctor and Skipper would be pleased to be remembered in this way.

Also in attendance was one of the charter members of the Burk's Falls Lions Club, Harvey Fowler, and former Scout, Everett Doherty of Huntsville. The latter spoke on behalf of the older generation of Burk's Falls Scouts. Doherty, who went to live with Frank and his wife Jean after he lost his father, explained that growing up in those days the way to get a boy into manhood was find a job in a lumber camp. "Not Frank. He believed in getting an education. He instilled in me the pride and good fortune to go out and get that education." Reflecting on Frank's untimely death on that spring day back in 1949, Doherty recalled that after his son had lapsed into a coma, Dr. Partridge arrived only to watch his son die, leaving behind a young widow and an infant daughter, Julie. "On the night of that terrible accident, we lost not one man, but five men: husband, father, Scouter, 4-H Leader, and town councillor."

After taking the tour of the camp grounds, former Burk's Falls Scout and King's Scout recipient, Murray Mackay of Hamilton, remarked that after fifty years, nothing much had changed, except the size of the trees—they'd gotten bigger. "I don't believe Dr. Partridge ever thought about how much fun he was creating for the boys of the neighbourhood by donating Green Bay to them." And fun they would have over the years, making their benefactor mighty proud.

Scouter Elwood Addison may not have had the opportunity in his youth to earn his King Scout's Award, but his scouting knowledge has led a succession of Scouts to the top award. Pictured here with "Addie," learning their lashings are two Burk's Falls Chief Scouts of 2005, Mary Kate Brown (foreground) and Sarah Hubbert. The Chief Scout Award replaced the King Scout and Queen Scout Award and is the highest honour a Scout can achieve.

Photograph by Astrid Taim

Since the 1940s, the 1st Burk's Falls Scouts have racked up an impressive list of recipients of the highest honour that can be achieved by a Scout. Recipients of the King's Scout Award (1909–57) after the Second World War were: (Dr.) Milton Wittick, Jackie Wilson, George Radford and Murray MacKay. The Queen's Scout's Award (1957–68) would go to: (Dr.) Jim Bell, Ian McNaughton, John Wilson, Eddie Bolton, Glenn Miller and Don Follick. In 1973, the Chief Scout Award was created by Governor General Roland Michener, who was then Chief Scout of Canada, to replace the two previous awards. The first Burk's Falls Scouts to receive the award in 1999 were Nick Kulchar of Katrine and James Trigg of Magnetawan. In 2005, three more Scouts would receive the Chief Scout Award, Mary Kate Brown of Sundridge, Brock Gould of Sprucedale and Sarah Hubbert of Strong Township (Pevensey).

For Elwood Addison, there would be some disappointments along the way, such as never attaining the King's Scout Award. "I had to go to work at an early age as we didn't have much money. So it didn't leave me any extra time after school. Sure wish I could have gotten that award." He needn't worry, as his guidance over the years of close to a dozen young people who did go on to receive the highest award in Scouting is a testament to his own skills as a Boy Scout.

For him, his most positive experience in Scouting was learning how to canoe. "Canoeing has always been a wonderful, relaxing activity in my life. I first learned how to paddle while in Scouts," he remarked. In 1959 when the troop had raised enough money, members purchased their first used canoe. "Jim Bell instructed us how to handle it. These skills have been passed on to the boys [now girls also], down through the years," explained Elwood. Today, the 1st Burk's

One of Elwood Addison's greatest pleasures these days is canoeing. It is a skill he learned as a youth with the 1st Burk's Falls Scouts. In the summer of 2002, the troop presented their favourite leader with his own canoe—aptly named *Addie*.

Falls Scouts own a number of canoes, all paid for through fundraising. As a special thank-you to their beloved Scout leader, a year or so following the cairn dedication, troop members presented a red canoe—*Addie*—to Elwood Addison. Although he has his own personal cedar-strip canoe, *Addie* is the one that he uses on a regular basis at camp.

Green Bay Scout Camp continues to be a special place not just for Elwood Addison, but for all for Scouting members. But it almost came to an end in the summer of 2004. Without any prior warning, Scouts Canada would declare that it was intent on disposing of about twenty Scout camps in Ontario—including Green Bay. The thinking behind the sell-off of properties according to Scouts Canada, was that perhaps some of the camps had become redundant while others still were becoming too much of a financial burden for the organization. The reality was that Scouts Canada was running a million-dollar-plus deficit in 2003–04. Despite the organization's promise that the money from the sale of any of its camps would go directly into enhancing programs and facilities at the nearest neighbouring camp, the public saw it differently. To the community, the sell-off of camps was seen as a "quick fix" to the organization's financial difficulty. As for the nearest Scout Camp to Green Bay, it would be hours away in either Haliburton or Owen Sound and cost members hundreds of dollars to attend—instead of just under $100 at the local camp.

Throughout its long history, the Green Bay Scout Camp had been supported by the community and in such a time of crisis, that community wasn't about to let the local Scout Troop down. Two lawyers would step forward to take on the case pro-bono, one in Toronto, the other locally. Burk's Falls lawyer Derek Miller, whose father Glenn, had not only been a member of the 1st Burk's Falls Scouts, but a Queen's Scout Award recipient as well, had a personal interest in saving the camp. The lawyers would argue that Scouts Canada may not have any authority to sell the camp, as it was a gift and there were strings attached. And since Scouts Canada had never made a financial contribution to Green Bay in its entire history, the camp could not be considered in any way a burden to the program. Petitions were circulated throughout the district and beyond, gathering thousands of signatures. CBC Radio One broadcast interviews with former Burk's Falls Scouts such as Everett Doherty, and Conservative Parry Sound Muskoka MPP Norm Miller would take Scouts Canada to task in writing for such an obvious money grab.

While waiting for the appeal date in the late fall, the Burk's Falls troop members would spend a very quiet time at the 2004 summer camp at Green Bay, wondering if it would be their last. For Elwood Addison, the very thought of losing the camp was almost too much to bear. Thankfully, with the overwhelming support of the community, including six area Lions Clubs who promised financial assistance for Green Bay, if Scouts Canada allowed the camp to remain, it did. Of course, many felt it did help that the surviving members of Dr. A.W. Partridge's family vowed to take Scouts Canada to court if the organization made any move to sell Green Bay.

Over the years, the good, and yes, even the bad times experienced by Burk's Falls Scouting, including the death of Frank Partridge and the almost sale of Green Bay have been carefully recorded by Elwood Addison. Photographs and newspaper clippings are all stored in countless albums, as well as the many notebooks in which he jotted down the achievements of the Scout troop.

Summing up his experiences, he said, "I have countless happy memories that I enjoy every time that I meet one of the former Scouts and we start to reminisce. Looking through these albums bring back many happy memories as well. Baden-Powell's teachings still enthrall thousands of youth worldwide. Youth leaders have an awesome responsibility. Let us never abuse it as we strive to set a living example to them. They are our future leaders."[1]

Kearney: Home of Ontario Baseball Champions

The Town of Kearney is proud of its sports heritage, particularly when it comes to the grand game of baseball. And little wonder. At the turn of the 20th century, amateur baseball in Canada had become all the rage and the Kearney men's baseball team was to win not just one Ontario championship title, but three in a row. The winning seasons were 1903, 1904 and 1905 respectively. It is truly sad that after one hundred years, there is no one around to remember anything about the opposing teams.

As for the local ball players, they would proudly sport the Kearney name on their jerseys, despite the fact there was no actual town as such. The settlement, located in Parry Sound District on the western boundary of Algonquin Park, wouldn't be incorporated as a town until 1908. For team manager, Irishman Robert McConkey Sr., there was a provincial championship title at stake. Since residents referred to their community as Kearney—that was fine by him—it would go on the jerseys. And as Irish luck would have it, his players were to grant him his wish, three times over.

It is not known exactly how McConkey got involved with the town's baseball team. Was it for the love of the game? The answer could be as simple as that. But in those early days of the 20th century, any sort of recreational activity was viewed by the settlers as a welcome relief from the hard monotonous daily grind. The diversions could be as simple as a community picnic, or as complicated as winning a provincial championship. Robert McConkey and his wife Sarah Hassard are listed among the very first homesteaders to settle Kearney, at nearby Sand Lake. A hard-working couple, they, along with their sons Robert Jr. and Chester, had a driving sense of how to win a ball game.

Now, more than one hundred years later a whole new generation is experiencing the thrill of McConkey's championship wins, thanks to the generosity of Chester McConkey's son Wilfred. Early in 2006, the then mayor of Kearney, Cliff Reeds, was approached by the family, wondering if the town would be interested in some early baseball memorabilia. Although the answer was a resounding "Yes," the inquiry itself wasn't by chance. On one of her most recent visits to Kearney, Wilfred's daughter Susan happened to stop in at the Kearney Community Centre and

Top: In order to get to Kearney, a traveller had to pass through Emsdale first. This small community remained fairly well established until at least the 1950s. This postcard shot was taken sometime in the 1920s, looking westward into the business section. In 1935, Emsdale was hit with one of its worst fires, destroying a major portion of its commercial sector. *Bottom*: In the 1920s, the Town of Kearney took some pride in having an orderly community. Looking southward, its main street may have been a dirt road and the homes and businesses lining it of frame construction, but it was still a thriving community. This postcard is interesting because it includes the town's once most popular hotel, the large three-storey building on the left known as the Kearney House. The hotel is long since gone.

in the main lobby she spotted a display case. There, front and centre, was the faded photograph of Robert McConkey's championship team of 1904. She immediately contacted her father. As Susan explained, "When my grandfather Chester passed away in 1972 at the age of eighty-two, I found some of his baseball gear collected together in a grip. No one had any idea what to do with it." Back in the earliest days of 1900, Chester had been one of his father's pitchers, as well as playing third baseman. Although his brother Robert was a member of their father's championship team, by that time Chester had already turned professional. For a short period of time, he was to play in the minor league for a team in Pincher Creek, Alberta.

The grip left to the McConkey family contained Chester's original Spalding mitt, a 1908 baseball, a series of championship medals, five baseball guide books dating from 1897 to 1943, an authenticated photograph from the 1911 World Series in New York and lastly, a souvenir Kearney stamp holder with period stamps. Chester had hung onto the stamp holder because his father had not only been the manager of the local baseball team, but the first postmaster when Kearney was incorporated as a town. As for the World Series photograph, it was purchased by Chester when he and teammates Bob Mann and Bill O'Neill went to New York to see the New York Giants play the Philadelphia Athletics. "The three of them had to stay an extra day in order to purchase a press photo of the game," said Susan. "Any

It was a proud moment for the McConkey family when they presented the Town of Kearney with historic baseball memorabilia from the early 1900s. Pictured here are Mary Ann Ross (left) and Susan Roncadin, with their uncle Wilfred McConkey, grandson of Robert McConkey. The baseball collection belonged to Robert McConkey's son, Chester. The presentation to the town was made in June 2006.

Photograph by Astrid Taim

The members of the 1904 baseball championship team from Kearney were fine-looking players. Pictured here is the team that won that first title. Front row (l–r): Wilmot Irwin (pitcher) and Wes Jordan (catcher and captain); centre row (l–r): Walter Irwin, William O'Neill, Ernie Craig (team mascot), Chas Rhodes and Dave W. Mark; back row (l–r): E. Barlow, Robert McConkey Sr. (manager), Robert McConkey Jr., Albert J. Woodruff (manager), Harvey S. Bell and Frank Prunty.

photographs that didn't make the newspapers were offered for sale." Of note, the Philadelphia Athletics would win the 1911 World Series by beating the New York Giants in six games, 4–2.

Although Robert McConkey Jr. would die of complications from pneumonia while still a relatively young man, Chester's love of the game never left him. He continued to play professionally until the Depression set in. When Chester decided to move his family to Sudbury, according to son Wilfred, he became the manager of the Falconbridge team and later became president of the Nicklebelt baseball league. Chester and his wife Theresa Agnes had three children, Maxwell, who was Susan and Mary Ann's father, Wilfred and Marion. It would be in June of 2006 that Wilfred McConkey and his wife Janet made the special trip from their home in Grosse Point, Michigan, to present the town with the historic baseball memorabilia. Wilfred was accompanied by his two nieces, Susan and her husband Rino Roncadin of Aurora, and Mary Ann Ross of Toronto. As a way of saying "thank-you," the municipality presented Wilfred with a commemorative afghan throw, depicting historic sites in Kearney.

Who were the members of the Kearney baseball team besides the two McConkey boys and their father? And who are the players in the photo of the 1904 championship team? Those that can be positively identified have been identified in the photograph of the championship team.

There are no doubts; they were a mighty fine group of players—a credit to Kearney.[1]

14
Sundridge and the Johnstone Story

At first glance one would never suspect that the booming grocery business in Sundridge got its start as a little bakeshop. Today, although it has new owners, the bright and airy IGA on Highway #11 stands as a testimonial to a progressive-thinking pioneer family, who for generations supplied the area's residents with all their grocery needs.

In 1895, when John Philemon Johnstone first arrived in the village, he sought out employment at J.C. Faulkner's bakeshop. The idea of one day owning his own business was so appealing that once J.P. settled down and married Amanda Mundt, the couple started their own shop in downtown Sundridge, known as Johnstone's Bakery. Over the years it grew to include more than just candies and baked goods—a whole line of groceries would become available. Maintaining its location in the village's business section, the bakeshop turned into a fledgling grocery store in the early 1920s. By the 1950s it was known as Johnstone's Food Market and was owned by J.P.'s son Fred and his wife Evelyn. Fortunately for area residents, as trends changed in market shopping, the Johnstones were up to the challenge.

There would be no need to travel great distances in search of a modern grocery store as in 1972, the family bought into the Independent Grocers Alliance (IGA). Johnstone's IGA became one of the first brand-name "chain" stores in Almaguin Highlands and ownership of the business was now in the hands of Fred and Evelyn's sons Bob (wife Arlene) and Dave (wife Pat). However, with the business taking off, the store soon outgrew the building it was in on the village's Main Street. It would be in 1978 that the Johnstones made the decision to move to a new location on the west side of Highway #11 that still allowed them to remain in Sundridge. Remodelling and small expansions within the store would continue over the next twenty years—all meeting with the approval of the shoppers. But as the turn of the 21st century loomed ahead, the older generation began pondering their future in the grocery business. A fire in the store almost sealed the family's fate, but by pulling up their bootstraps they managed one final expansion. Then, in 2001, the Johnstone family decided it really was time to hang up the aprons and retire, selling the business to Joan and Paul Byrnes of North Bay. They may be out of the business, but are certainly not forgotten. Here is the Johnstone story.

Twelve years before J.P. Johnstone arrived in the small settlement by the shores of Stony Lake, his future in-laws, the Mundt family, were already cropping a small property just to the north. However, it seemed young Amanda Mundt had other ideas. She had no intention of spending her life on a farm. Hired on as a seamstress at Whitby's Tailor Shop, she would walk the three miles to town, each way, on a daily basis. Then, in 1889, when Sundridge was officially incorporated as a village, Whitby's shop was taken over by the Riddell family, who changed the name to Riddell's Tailor Shop. A few years later Amanda, still working there as a seamstress, would meet J.P.

Their courtship was brief and the couple were married in 1896 at the Methodist Church manse and was officiated by Rev. C.W. Reynolds, with Katie Hardy (Buchanan) as Amanda's only attendant. Following the wedding, J.P. and Amanda took up residence on Mill Street and became neighbours to the Carter (no relation to John Carter and Mary Anderson Carter of an earlier section) and A. Burnsides families. With a wife to support and a future to plan, J.P. went to work as a cook in the local lumber camps, arriving home with the spring break-up. This pattern of life continued for a few years until the couple had saved enough money to purchase Mr. Carter's confectionary store. Because her husband seemed more interested in the out-of-doors, Amanda took charge of the store, and immediately added baked goods to the line of

The Village of Sundridge continued to grow throughout the early decades of the twentieth century, adding more businesses to the main street. Sundridge Hardware, pictured here on the left, survives today under the same family as Kidd's Home Hardware. Only the location has changed, with the business now located on Highway 11. Johnstone's General Merchants on the east side of the street eventually became Johnstone's IGA. It too moved to the highway, with the Johnstone family selling the business only a few years ago.

candy and other sweets. Not content with remaining just a sweets shop, the Johnstones would later add on a barbershop, with J.P. taking on the position of the village barber.

It was now the early 20th century and Sundridge was continuing to grow. Charles Wisser built both a home along with a harness and shoe repair shop on the east side of street, not far from the bakery, while the Carters turned over the operation of the post office to a Mr. Sidewand. During the first decade of the 1900s, Bell Telephone installed the first switchboard in Sundridge—in the Johnstone Bakery. Amanda Johnstone's children remember quite vividly their mother operating the switchboard. "Nine o'clock was closing time, but no matter what the hour, when the buzzer rang, someone always answered," said daughter Lucy (Rennie). "By this time we were a family of five children, keen to pick up new ideas"—meaning that after hours the children were the ones answering the switchboard. As Lucy would recall, it also paid to have a mother who ran a candy store. "You can be sure we never left for school without our pockets bulging with cent candies. Often a few of the more expensive chocolates would also be pocketed."

In writing down the family history, Lucy would remember with some fondness, the large glass case that held the one-cent candies. "Once the front glass was broken, making it much more handy for us children. Father was quite stern with us, but I always felt mother had a kinder, understanding way with us. She always had a smile for everyone, and was a good listener." As children, the Johnstone clan could get into all sorts of mischief, sometimes dragging their friends along with them. As Lucy would write, "I well remember finding a large fresh pineapple in a crate out in the shed where boxes were stored. Bertha Dunbar and I ate it all. We couldn't swallow properly for a day or so. Mother understood."

Although J.P. and Amanda would sell the bakery, building and all, in 1912 to George Kemp, they would turn around and use the money to buy another store from a Mr. French. Located across the road on the corner of Main and Paget streets, their new location would also house the Bell Telephone switchboard. It was here that the Johnstones would launch their grocery store. But, it would be Amanda that once again was left in charge while her husband continued his outdoor endeavours. The shingle outside the new store would reflect the chain of command—A.E. Johnstone's, not J.P. Johnstone's.

If J.P. was said to have one true passion—it was horses. So when the nearby livery stable was offered for sale, he bought it. As his children would recall, their father had many long cold drives during the winter months. He would be all wrapped up in a huge black bearskin coat with hot bricks at his feet, and driving "a spanking team." All his customers sitting in the cutter were kept equally warm, all tucked up in buffalo robes. J.P. put Duncan Tobodio in charge of looking after the livery stable horses.

Because horse races were very popular those days, both at fall-fair time and out on Lake Bernard during the winter months, J.P. not only entered horses, but bet on them as well. As daughter Lucy remembers, "One horse my father raced and won many prizes with was called Roan Billy. Another horse was called Black Babe and was owned by Willard Lang."

Around that same time, "Father purchased a large launch, and booms of logs were towed across the lake, and scows brought pulpwood over," recalled Lucy. "We [Johnstone children] had many picnics over at Flannigan's Landing with him." It meant leaving their mother behind to look after the store. Amanda Johnstone certainly never seemed to complain. In those early days, running a general store meant trade by barter as ready cash was scarce. In fact, three-quarters of the purchases were made on credit. One item customers frequently used for barter was the berry crop. The Johnstone children were expected to work after school filling baskets with blueberries, and covering tubs of raspberries with mosquito netting before hauling them off to the railway station to be shipped off to Toronto to a jam factory. Fortunately, the station was right in the village, not too far from the Johnstone's store.

According to Lucy Johnstone, "One learns much about human nature in a village general store, and can soon sense the competitive spirit. There was no price fixing. Few groceries were packaged." Since a variety of goods came in bulk and were, in turn, sold by weight, it would compel Lucy to write, "I well remember the coal oil pump at the back of the store, and just dreaded to see

While his wife, Amanda, looked after running the family's general store, J.P. Johnstone pursued his outdoor interests. Pictured here in front of the business is Johnstone's fall hunting party and its bounty. Members of the group that can be identified include (from left): J.P. Johnstone, J.P. Johnstone Jr., Fred Johnstone, Fred English, unidentified, Ray Hall (in back), unidentified. The two children in the front are also Johnstone family members. The name of the gentleman kneeling is not known.

customers come in with empty vinegar jugs, or ask for a piece of salt pork, as that meant a trip away down in the cellar." Interestingly, the Johnstone's front parlour served for a while as the office for the village's first dentist. That is, until proper accommodations could be secured.

The Johnstone family home was attached to the business. It had nine rooms, all stretched out along the side of the store, with a big back kitchen. In behind the store numerous storage sheds were scattered along the property, ending up with a barn down on the lake. It was here where, according to Lucy, the delivery horses were kept. When farmers came in from a distance to do business at the store, their horses had a warm stall waiting for them in the barn where they were also fed and watered.

J.P. Johnstone's love of the out-of-doors would mean numerous hunting and fishing parties (in season), with a favourite stopping place being his own camp, "Hop-To-It." Here he and Sidney Smith supposedly had an encounter with a black bear. "There sure were some tall stories told," said Lucy. "Father could spin yarns with the straightest face." One of her favourite tales is as follows: "Father was out hunting and got lost and climbed a hollow stump to get his bearings. He fell down inside and lost all hope of ever getting out. After a while he heard a lot of scratching, and realized something had blocked the light at the top. A black bear had backed down inside, and he grabbed the hind of the bear, hanging on for dear life. The bear quickly started climbing out, and Father got to the top and safely back to camp." It appears that after the hunters returned to Toronto, the story came out in the *Toronto Daily Star*, along with an illustration. Before long it appeared in a British newspaper as well, and J.P. received three offers for the copyright, from three different magazines. Or so the story goes—John Philemon Johnstone was renowned for being a good entertainer.

Since he owned a considerable acreage of land along the western shore of Stony Lake/Lake Bernard, J.P. decided one day to build a couple of cottages. When not rented out, the grounds were used for Sunday school picnics. "I can still see very tall Miss Sarah Hall, managing the children. On Saturday night after closing the store, we [children] would all pile into the delivery wagon and go to the cottage for the weekend. That is a cherished memory of my childhood days." In later years the Johnstone cottages would be purchased by Dale and Algie Campbell of Brampton.

With the Johnstone's store such a focal point in the community, the family catered church picnics, both at the Pevensey United Church as well as at the one at Bloomfield. "We were up early getting the ice cream packed. Mother was making the lemonade in ice cream cans and packing candies and bananas in the wagon. Then we were off. Either Bob Minorgan or Alex McMurchy was on hand to help. The picnic stand was built under trees, and we always hoped there would be a good branch sticking out to hold the bunch of bananas," Lucy recalled.

During the war years, 1914–18, Amanda Johnstone was the president of the local chapter of the Red Cross Society. Both the society's workroom and meeting space were at the Presbyterian Church, conveniently located between the store and the hotel. As well, the 162nd Battalion trained at Paget's farm located just east of the village. Not only was Village of Sundridge considerably livelier during the First World War, but the activity also brought in extra business to the Johnstone's store. It was most unfortunate that a fire broke out in 1917 and destroyed

Johnstone's Tourist Camp would become one of the most popular vacation spots in Sundridge. This is a photograph of a postcard from the era. Although not named here, there was no mistaking whose campground it was. The tourist camp was located on the shores of Lake Bernard.

the business just when they were booming. However, the store was rebuilt quickly and Amanda continued to run things by herself. By 1923 she had an extra pair of hands as son Fred, now nineteen years of age, was only too willing to get started in the business. He would first manage and later own the family's grocery store. After forty years, he would turn the store over to his sons, Bob and Dave.

As for J.P. Johnstone, while the family was looking after the business, he gave his attentions to municipal politics and was instrumental, some say, in having the government dock built. He served on council and ultimately became Sundridge's reeve, but the out-of-doors would come beckoning once again.

In 1923, J.P. purchased the Sutherland Innes property, which then consisted of nothing more than a stone building and acres of swampy land. Slowly but surely he would turn it into Johnstone's Tourist Camp. Year after year J.P. brought in landfill and cleared more space, before putting up a few cottages. During the summer season, Johnstone's Tourist Camp was awash in tents, one could say almost becoming its own little village. Tenting was free. Otherwise, rates were $1 a night for bed and breakfast. If the family was small and looked prosperous, they were charged $2 for a cottage. If it was a large family, J.P. would charge only a $1. Lucy would recall that for years after, people wrote or stopped in to say how much they had enjoyed their vacation

Sundridge and the Johnstone Story 145

Postcards were a popular way to promote local business. Pictured here are two views of Johnstone's Tourist Camp in Sundridge. Vacationers in the 1920s and early 1930s had their choice of cabins or tents. J.P. Johnstone adored large families and gave them a cheaper rate.

Courtesy of the Burk's Falls and District Museum

there with their families. "The dances in the camp's large hall were famous for miles around." Ten years later in 1934, J.P. Johnstone purchased the house and property next to his tourist camp and he and Amanda moved out of the store into their new home.

When Fred took over his mother's business, the grocery store carried on much the same way Amanda had run it. Johnstone's Food Market, as it was now called, continued to keep up with the trends and to attract new customers. Running the store with his wife and family wasn't Fred's only interest. During the 1940s he became involved with politics and ran, unsuccessfully, as a candidate for the federal Progressive Conservatives in the Parry Sound riding. He also became one of the founding members of the Sundridge Lions Club. In the 1950s, he was a member of the local board of education. Fred's love of curling saw him join the North Bay Granite Club, where he was "skip," and go on to win several trophies. Over the next decade he was the president of the Sundridge Beavers hockey team. It was in the 1960s, during Fred's tenure, that the Sundridge Beavers were the Ontario Hockey League Association's Intermediate C champions. Fred's son Ross played on the team, as did a number of other well-known local men.

Fred's sons Bob and Dave took over Johnstone's Food Market in 1963. Within ten years, it became known as Johnstone's IGA. With the move to a new location on the highway in 1978, there were two expansions, one in 1983 and again in 1990. Fred Johnstone, now affectionately known as "Grandpa" by area residents, continued to spend about four to six hours a day at the grocery store. Until 1996, his main job was tending the Garden Centre.

The 1990s were the twilight years for Fred. By 1994, he was the last surviving Charter member of the Sundridge Lions Club. In July 1997, after seventy-one years of marriage, his wife Evelyn Summers passed away. Fred would follow her one year later. His death came at the age of ninety-four, on April 14, 1998, at the Eastholme Home for the Aged in Powassan.

Yes, Sundridge may have been the home of the famous Beavers Hockey team, but the village also had its fair share of NHL players—including Greg deVries, Fred's grandson. DeVries brought the Stanley Cup home to Sundridge after his team, the Colorado Avalanche, won it in 2001. Other NHL players to come from Sundridge include Greg Theberge, as well as the father and son team of Ron and Bob Atwell, the father and son team of Bill Sr. and Bill Jr. McCreary, and Keith McCreary—brother of Bill Sr. Keeping it all in the family, the Atwells are related through marriage to the McCrearys. The most famous NHL player to come from Sundridge is, of course, Bucko MacDonald. He spent thirteen years in the NHL, winning three Stanley Cups, 1936 and 1937 with the Detroit Red Wings and in 1942 with the Toronto Maple Leafs. MacDonald was also named as an all-star NHL defenseman in the 1940s, before making the move into politics—spending twelve years in the House of Commons.[1]

Not bad, all things considered, for the community by the lake—sunny Sundridge.

Galna Bridge: The Bridge That Will Stand Forever

On Thursday, October 17, 1912, the same year in which the *Burk's Falls Arrow* office was built, the Galna Bridge in Burk's Falls was opened. Spanning the Magnetawan River above the dam, it was named in honour of John Galna who at that time was the MPP for the Parry Sound District. To commemorate the auspicious occasion, an *Arrow* contributor who signed himself "Pontifex Minimus," penned a poem entitled, " The Bridge That Will Stand Forever."[1] The opening verse is as follows:

> Once we went scrambling down the hill
>   And over the railway track,
> Where an old bridge swayed beneath the wheel
>   With many an ominous crack,
> Till we thought that surely horse and cart,
>   Would plunge in the foaming river;
> But how we behold with thankful heart
>   A bridge that will stand forever.

Sadly, after years of neglect, the Galna Bridge was demolished on December 11, 1987. It wouldn't be the only bridge to span the Magnetawan River in Burk's Falls. During the Depression, the Armstrong Bridge on Highway #11 was constructed in 1938 and named after Dr. Armstrong. The physician's father, Sheriff Armstrong, was reportedly one of the early settlers in the area.

Seven years after the Galna Bridge came down, the Welcome Centre and the Heritage River Walk were officially opened on September 4, 1994. The covered footbridge leading to the Centre on Highway #520 is located just below the dam. As for the Heritage River Walk, it stretches from the racetrack on the arena grounds to the new bridge. Rich in history, the nature trail harkens back to the turn of the century when on April 15, 1901, the Magnetawan River Railway Company was formed. The company decided that a rail line should be built

Top: The dam at Burk's "Falls," photograph taken circa 1912. In the background one can just catch a glimpse of a footbridge and the footings of the Galna Bridge, named in honour of John Galna, at that time the MPP for the District of Parry Sound. ***Bottom***: Just four years after it was opened, the Galna Bridge in Burk's Falls was used as a crossing for the 162nd Battalion, which was part of the huge contingent of Canadian troops sent to Europe in 1916. Composed of men from the Parry Sound District, the company passed through Burk's Falls on a route march from its base at Sundridge.

"For King and Empire" is how young Canadian men viewed the call to arms during the Great War. In this photograph, believed to have been taken of the local enlisted men from Burk's Falls, a little girl is dressed as Britannia, complete with her white robes, a Corinthian helmet and holding Poseidon's three-pronged trident. Britannia is seen as a national personification of the United Kingdom.

connecting the Burk's Falls station on the Grand Trunk railway line and the village itself. This steam-operated railway system was mainly used as a freight spur, transporting goods from the river to the railway station.

Today, the historic spur line has been enhanced to provide visitors with a scenic walking trail. It provides a walk back in time to a place where a way of life, like bridges, was supposed to last forever.

Epilogue

Almaguin Highlands—just where did the name come from? According to a 1960s newscap in the *Burk's Falls Arrow* and *Sundridge Echo* (later the *Almaguin News* (Almaguin Publishing (1988) Ltd.), the name Almaguin evolved out of a late 1950s battle for tourist dollars within the District of Parry Sound. Unfortunately, fifty years later, that battle has not subsided as East Parry Sound, which Almaguin Highlands embraces, appears to be in peril with a proposed assimilation into the more northern Blue Sky Region, touted by its proponents as "bigger and better." Blue Sky was developed to serve the economic interests of the North Bay-Mattawa area.

But, going back in time, members of the Magnetawan River and Lakes Tourist Association felt that the only way to give local tourism the boost it needed in the 1950s was to create an identity that would clearly distinguish the east side of the district from the west. It would be the summer of 1958 that the search commenced for a new name. To reach the largest number of people possible, a contest was run in the *Burk's Falls Arrow*. The association was looking for something unique, a name that would clearly define the region in the minds of prospective vacationers—a region bounded by the southern community of Novar, the northern Town of Powassan, Algonquin Park to the east and the Village of Dunchurch on the western boundary. In other words, they were looking for a name that would be instantly recognizable and help tourists in separating the two sides of the district when it came to choosing a travel destination. After all, the Town of Parry Sound, conveniently located on the shores of Georgian Bay, had anchored the district long enough. Now was the time to break away and form a new distinct identity.

Name-The-Area-Contest offered $50 as the top prize and attracted more than 100 entries. Interestingly enough, it would be a tourist who ultimately came up with the winning entry. Jean Sutherland of the Forest Hill area of Toronto submitted the name "Almaguin—Algonquin-Magnetawan Highlands." Sutherland chose "AL," from the word Algonquin to identify the indigenous tribe whose hunting grounds were now a tourist haven. "MAG" stood for the Magnetawan River which cut through the heart of the Highlands and "UIN," pronounced "WIN," was supposedly added to create an aboriginal flavour. "WIN, it was a 'good old Indian name'—the same as Muskoka and Algoma—manufactured by the white man," stated the *Arrow*.

Sutherland's winning entry was chosen by a committee of eight area businessmen. Representing the South River Chamber of Commerce were Ron Hall, Clarke Stevenson and Stuart Dennis. The Sundridge Chamber of Commerce was represented by Earl Anderson, Bill Vrooman and D.R. Kidd. Finally, representing the tourism association were Morrison "Morry" Barr, the *Arrow's* editor and soon-to-be publisher of the newly minted *Almaguin News*, along with Harvey Raaflaub.

At last, the breathtaking hills of Almaguin Highlands were now open for a new era in tourism, one that has lasted right into the 21st century. With sparkling waterways criss-crossing the vast lakeland area, the region offers everything from pristine beaches to white-water rapids and some of the best traditional fishing grounds in the province. Covering an area that begins just north of Muskoka's Town of Huntsville, visitors are warmly greeted by Perry Township's two main communities, Novar and Emsdale. And along the ninety-kilometre strip of Highway #11, to the border of Nipissing District, are the many picturesque hamlets, villages and towns that continue to stand as testimonials to the Europeans who first settled the region more than 125 years ago. But there is, in fact, more than first meets the eye. Stretching outwards from the highway corridor—to the eastern boundary of Algonquin Park and then westward towards Georgian Bay for approximately fifty kilometres, exists a splendid wilderness area just waiting to be explored.

Today, with the provincial government committed to the completion of Highway #11 as a four-lane route north to North Bay, getting to the heart of the Almaguin Highlands is so much easier than in those earlier times that make up so much of the content of this sequel to the author's first book on the district, *Almaguin: A Highland History*. The area has a rich and colourful history, largely under-recorded until recently, but now taking its rightful place in the documentation of Ontario's story.

Appendix A: Poems and Songs of Clarence Brazier

The Ballad of Clarence Brazier (In honour of his 100th birthday)

    Come listen to a story of a Timmins Pioneer
    His name is Clarence Brazier and to him we'll raise a beer.
    He grew up in old Sundridge town where life was really tough,
    That made him into iron man, he's not filled up with fluff.
    ...iron man Brazier
    Born on the shores of Lake Bernard, here he first had birthday cake.
    He then moved to Magnetawan and lived on Whalley Lake.
    A farm his parents George and Mae bought for 500 bucks
    To farm and raise their six children they needed lots of luck.
    ... grew up on the Mag
    But luck was not forthcoming and a tragedy took place
    George Brazier lost his eyesight when rock blew up in his face.
    This left a mom with six young kids to house and clothe and feed,
    And Clarence from the age of six worked hard to meet this need.
    ... no time for school
    Clarence and his young siblings did chores and cut the hay.
    They tried to turn work into fun but rarely got to play.
    In summer they picked blueberries from morning until dark,
    And sold them to Toronto where folks ate them in the park.
    ... hundreds of baskets of blueberries
    At age fourteen this lad left home, he worked the lumber then.
    He also worked on river drives and entertained the men.
    He moved to Timmins and to work at McIntyre Mine,
    He bought a farm, found Angela and strung her quite a line.
    ... robbed the cradle he did

Ange gave birth to a son named Ron he was a lovely child.
How sad to have him die so young the pain near drove them wild.
He was the only son they had, they love him to this day,
He never got a chance to help his dad bring in the hay.
... a sad time for Mom and Dad
They had three daughters in a row that kept them very busy
Pearl and Doris and then Janet, now they're getting dizzy.
Clarence worked hard in the gold mine and he bought himself a farm.
He moved the whole gang out of town he didn't give a darn.
... log cabin... Horseshoe Lake
Now the baby of the family, she was born in '43
Named Irene and Archie, she filled out the family tree.
Her best friend was her border collie with the name of Queenie.
If she had to get along without him she became a meanie.
... and Prince and Polly, our horses
Clarence worked real hard to feed and clothe his growing family
Put up with lots of squabbles, carried out the pots of pee
Raised beef and chickens, grew some spuds, cut trees down when he could.
And after dark he went to town, delivered cords of wood.
... lots of pee pots
For many years he nursed his wife and helped her live at home.
He had to cook and help her dress, her hair he had to comb.
He never once complained about the chores he did with cheer,
She was his darling and he'll always miss his little dear.
...the love of his life
As Clarence had to work hard from the tender age of six
He never learned to read or write, this problem he just fixed.
At the age of 93 he thought "I can't leave this till later,"
And now you'll find him reading books and also the newspaper.
... learning to read at 93
In '95 he left the north, moved south with Doe and Jim.
We hope he didn't think there'd be a free ride then for him
He didn't get to fill his face in a food trough all for free,
He continued yet to hoe and till and cut down the odd tree.
... Cut all the firewood until he was 98 and grows 100 quarts of raspberries.
The fact that Dad learned late to read brought him publicity.
He's starred in many newspapers and on the CBC.
At Aurora Public School, he spoke to many kids and teachers.
Toronto Star and *Huntsville Forester* had him as their feature.
... the Poster Boy for Muskoka Literacy Council

Now Clarence runs the township on a brand new ATV
He's made of sturdy stuff this man, he's not like you and me.
He cuts down wood and tends his garden, handing out the stuff.
He says he's ready now to quit, he says he's had enough.
... retirement at just 100, no way
Today we all have gathered here to wish you all the best
You've reached your hundredth birthday and you've had no time to rest.
Our deep respect we give to you as you enjoy this day
Just don't think you can rest up now, get to work and earn your pay.
... we love you Dad. You're the best
Everyone joins in Happy Birthday.

More Clarence Brazier Poems and Songs

At the age of 100, Clarence Brazier can be forgiven for not quite remembering which ones of the following poems and songs he penned in his youth and which ones were historic to the times he lived. When he first walked into the Canada Pine Lumber Camp, he spotted six fellows coming out. "The turnover was terrific," he recalled. To keep the men occupied Clarence, along with his friends drivers Jack Russell and Henry Welsh came up with the idea of starting an entertainment troupe. "We had tricks, stories and square dancing," he laughed. "Sure kept the spirits up." By entertaining the men on weekends—Saturday nights and a bit earlier on Sundays, the turnover of men dropped by over 50 percent. And the payback to Clarence and his partners was huge. Clarence, Jack and Henry were paid a bonus of $15 a month each, for the next three months. "The Canada Pine Lumber Company was glad to pay us," says Clarence. "They didn't lose as many men." And the bonus was on top of the wages, which were just $35 a month. There was lots of fun too, in entertaining," he smiled. In fact, he liked it so much he continued to sing songs and entertain the men as he went from logging camp to logging camp.

The following verses reflect the earlier life and times of Clarence Brazier, ones that he still remembers.

Florella (Clarence Brazier's favourite song)

When in down in yon lone valley where the violets fade and bloom
There lies my own Florella in her dark and silent tomb.
She died not broken-hearted, with no lingering sickness fell
But in one moment parted from her friends she loved so well.

Last night the moon shone brightly and the stars were shining too
When into her cottage window her treacherous lover flew.

He said come let us wander down through the forest deep
And undisturbed we'll ponder and we'll name our wedding day.

Way deep into the valley he led his love so dear
She says it is for you dear only, that I have wandered here
The way was dark and dreary and I am afraid to stay
Dear Edward I would rather that we retrace the way.

Retrace your way, no never, no more these woods you'll roam
So say goodbye forever to parents, friends and home
In these woods I have you, and from me you cannot fly
No mortal arms can save you, Florella you must die.

Down on her knees before him she pleaded for her life
But deep into her bosom, he plunged that fatal knife
What have I done dear Edward that you should take my life?
I never have deceived you and would have been your wife.

Goodbye kind friends and parents, your faces I'll see no more
Long, long you'll wait my coming at the little cottage door.

Lumberjack Song

Two lumberjacks, Jack Russell and Henry Welsh, came to the farm, looking for a chore boy to work in the lumber camp. In the fall they came back to get him and they went to the bush. According to Clarence, "The guys picked me up in Sundridge, to take me to work, I was too young to go alone. I made up a song about the walking boss that very first winter."

As Clarence remembers, it went something like this:

A year last October that I first went astray
We were drinking up booze in the town of North Bay
We hired with an agent who treated us fine
To cut down the timber for the Sweder Mills Pine[1]

We then met our walker, Jim Ludgate by name
A burling big Scotsman without any brain
Then right after dinner he said it was time
We were dangling along for the Sweder Mills Pine

Now the days they were long and the hour was late
We covered that trail at a terrible rate
The roads they were muddy and the hills hard to climb
On the trail that we took to the Sweder Mills Pine

When we got to the half-way it was then time to dine
They fed us some prunes from the Sweder Mills Pine

That night we arrived in camp Number One
I sure was delighted my journey was done.
They put me in a bunk with young Jerry O'Brien
He's a boy that cuts trail for the Sweder Mills Pine

Then early next morning about break of day
They put us in the bush at a dollar a day
The days they were long and the weather was fine
And I pulled that old fiddle for the Sweder Mills Pine

When the winter was over and the logs were all down
They gave us our checks and we hit for the "Sound"
We spent all our money we had a good time
We went back on the drive for the Sweder Mills Pine

The Buck Deer

Near the Town of Spence,[2] my boys. I've often heard them say
There dwelled a wild buck, and there he did lay.
He was hunted by brave Isaac, William, James and Joe
And none of them could shoot that buck when he was on full go.
Brave Isaac came home one night drunk on the booze
He said he shoot the buck any day that you choose
Early next morning about break of dawn
There was a firing of guns and yelping of hounds.
Such a noise as that was I had not heard before
You'd think that the Devil himself was at poor Isaac's door.
The buck he did run 'til he nearly was done
He ran to the water's edge and saw that wouldn't do
As Squire Nelson he was there with his tin canoe.
The buck turned around against that hard frozen shale,

He said to Squire Nelson, kiss under my tail.
Isaac shot the buck dead, laid him out on the floor
To his loving wife he said, I'll hunt deer no more.

The Shanty Man

I've been a jolly young shanty man and never took care of my life
I travelled this wide world all over and every darn town had a wife
But now that I'm dead and gone under all this puts an end to my life
I don't need no weeping and wailing, just do a good turn for my wife.
Yes, do a good turn for my wife, boys, she's the only darn thing that I crave
Just wrap me up in my old shanty blankets and fiddle and dance on my grave
And as you go fiddling and dancing along, may the people all say you've gone mad.
Take a drink! Here's to a true shanty lad.

The Travelling Salesman

We'll travel on through Ryerson
And around to the Township of Spence
Around by the Mag and home with my Jag
Oh, my, what an enormous expense.
I met Mrs. White on the Whirlpool Bridge
And what do you think she said?
She's going to be wed to Charlie, she said
And he's gone for the new suit of clothes.
I met Billy Ross, he put away my hoss
And asked me what farmer I robbed.
I've not robbed a thing since I left old Katrine,
I'm just going out on the job.

Whoa, Mule, Whoa

"A favourite song of mine," says Clarence Brazier. "I like mules I have a little bit of that breed in me."

I bought a mule on a market day, a mule and a cart combined
He was spavined on his two hind legs and both of his eyes were blind

You could knock a fly off his left ear while riding down the hill
I was bound to have a mate for him if it costs me a dollar bill.

"Whoa, mule, whoa," why don't you hear me holler?
Tie a knot at the end of his tail or he'll go through the collar.

Why don't you put him on the track, why don't you let him go?
Every time you take him out, it's "Whoa, mule, whoa!"
I took my girl out for a ride, that mule commenced to balk
Threw her out upon the road and tore her brand-new socks.

That girl she swore she'd have revenge, but it all was settled quick
That mule he up with both hind legs and today that girl is sick
I took that girl home upon my back and flung her in the bed
Put a mustard plaster on her back and another one on her head.

The doctor he was called upon and pronounced her very low
All that poor little girl could say today, is "Whoa, mule, whoa."

Appendix B: "Trouble on the Tote Road" by Everett Kirton

Trouble on the Tote Road

    Stuck in a hole on the Portage Road
        With a wheel bogged out of sight,
    A greenhorn skinner with a six-horse team
        Watched the dusk merge into night.
    He was far from camp, he was out of grub
        He had yelled till his lungs were sore;
    Not a horse of the six would tighten a tug
        They had pulled till they would pull no more.

    When around that bend by the Big Pine Tree
        Came a string team swing along;
    And the man on the load filled the woods as he passed
        With a rollicking log camp song.
    "Hello there, kid. You're some stuck."
        As he slid from his seat to the ground.
    "Let me take a hand at that Dead-Head Bunch,"
        Then he took a smooch around.

    A-lifting a collar to straighten a pad,
        A-buckling a hame strap tight.
    Then he climbed to the seat with a lilt to his lips,
        And a shift to his old clay pipe.
    A bunch of the ribbons he pulled off the brake
        And straightened them one by one.

Then he spoke to the leader, "Tread in on that paint,
    You bald-headed Son of a Gun."

"What's that leader's name? Come alive, there, Pete."
    And he dropped the shag with a bang.
"Stand away from that pole, you Soft-Horned Cow,
    Or I'll skin you alive. Ho, Hang."
"Oh, the line is on the pointer's hame.
    Get out of the road. Gee. Gee."
"Gee off you leaders, get in at the point,
    Now steady, you've shook her free."
"Is she clear there now? No. Well, I'll hit her again.
    WHOA till I make you swing."
"And I'll take her away with a bone in her teeth,
    Or I'll make the rigging sing."

"Now, steady," he said, "tighten up there, boys.
    Take care there boys, get away."
He sent them "HAW" as he dropped the bud
    On the big cold-shouldered bay.
The wheelers dropped till their bellies dragged.
    One slipped, but came up again.
The leaders hung like a pup to a root
    Till the pointers took the strain.
With a lurch and a jerk and a "steady boys,"
    "You've rolled her high and dry."
    "You could pull the pole from any old rig,
If you would only get down and try."[1]

Appendix C: Selected Writings by Richard Thomas

1. This Time—Let's Do Better

> Per capita economic growth 1981 for Newfoundland   3.5%
> per capita economic growth 1981 for Ontario   0.4%
> *Conference Board of Canada Economic Forecast January, 1981*

Who thought the day would ever come? Ontario has taken some rough body blows lately, declining economic growth, young people heading west for work, tourism struggling, farms disappearing, empty schoolrooms in one place and overcrowding in another. Hospital facilities are inadequate, and care for the elderly is insufficient. More than 2,000 Ontario lakes, plus the forests around them, are noticeably suffering from Acid Rain.

All of these problems could be seen coming years ago. Good management by a lean and serious government could have prevented the effects of all or most of them.

We can recover, rebuild, and mend. We can go on to restore Ontario's strength. But it will take the best thought and work from all of us PLUS the kind of vision and efficiency we have not had from an Ontario government in too many years.

With help from neighbours here at home, I've been working on some very promising approaches for us in Parry Sound. After four years on the Perry Township council it was obvious to me that we needed economic self reliance. I found some willing helpers and the Algonquin West Credit Union was born. Now it has over one million dollars in assets and serves 1,500 people in Perry, McMurrich, and Armour Townships, Kearney and Burk's Falls. It's a big step toward controlling our economic destiny.

I've been working at developing clean, renewable fuels that we can produce ourselves, and also ship to the south from Parry Sound. Chances are, I'll be driving on fuel alcohol that we can make here, when you see me next. Keep your eye open for "The Little Red Car."

I take some pride, too, in having helped to stave some problems. Along with many district reeves and councilors I worked hard to defeat the Red Book recommendations for municipal restructuring.

When I came back home in 1969 I thought I'd do a lot of swimming, fishing and skiing. It turned out there were a few jobs to do first. I think my next job is to help a Liberal government to straighten things out in Queen's Park.

The Ontario Liberals have plans and policies for all areas. Many of them they put before the legislature, only to have them turned down, or just partly adopted. You'll be hearing more from me about those plans in my next letter. I'll be looking forward to your questions when I see you.

Yours truly,
Richard Thomas

2. And Another Thing....

The April 5, 2006, edition of the *Almaguin News* (*Almaguin Publishing* (1989) Limited) was the last time Richard Thomas's column "And Another Thing" appeared in print. The weeks leading up to Thomas's untimely death on February 22, 2006, the *News* reprinted his columns from earlier years.

The last *And Another Thing*...people would read is from the *Almaguin News*, April 14, 1987:

This is Dumb Question column #14. At thirteen weeks, TV sitcoms call it a season and go into reruns.

I can't do that. I'd be embarrassed. After all Ralph Bice has been taking us *Along the Trail* ever since he guided Captain Noah to a safe landing on Mount Ararat, which I understand is somewhere east of Kearney in Algonquin Park.

Do I want to pause for a kind of quarterly review though. So this week's question is, "What am I doing here?"

I am ruminating. That word delights me by being exactly right. Sheep ruminate. So do goats and cows. Cud chewers are called ruminants. They crop up grass and leaves and swallow the stuff barely bruised. When they've tucked away a good load they start the serious stuff back up for more chewing. It will pass back and forth between jaws and stomachs (four of them) until the nourishment has been ruminated out of it.

The leftovers are dropped on the pasture from the other end to help new grass to grow. Ruminants can digest protein out of cellulose, which is more than you and I can do.

I am an information ruminant. It takes me several tries to get an idea chewed ready for digestion. In the end, whether it is the protein or the leftover which appears in these columns, I am not ready to debate in open forum. I believe there is a running theme in my ruminations though. It is that as a society we humans deserve better of each other than we are delivering. The thoughtful, humane, and compassionate parts of us are being outshouted by the clangor of material progress like Mozart at a rock concert.

I have harped on about the destructive folly of our consumer economy. Why wouldn't I? We are production and consumption junkies. We seem to believe that the answer to every problem is to increase industrial production. As the production increases, so does the rate of suicides, especially among adolescents. Toxic waste overload builds up. And the wealth we think we create, winds up in fewer hands as the tragic gap widens between those who have too much and those who struggle for barely enough. In wistful nostalgia many of us try to recall different times when we liked each other more and had more time to help. Nowadays we might drop money in the pot to help a burned out family, but few of us gather for a rebuilding bee.

The example of Mennonites after the Barrie tornado in '85 shines out. While politicians vied to promise more money and some people schemed scams to get more than their share, the Mennonites showed up with their toolboxes, uninvited from down Waterloo way. They were there to help.

"I know of no way to accumulate material wealth without abusing other people along the way. There is dignity in wanting to preserve a world in which morning air smells sweet and the water is pure."

Dignity. That may be the key. What is dignity to you? In the main, I think it is something we confer on each other. The Mennonites gave dignity to the devastated people of Barrie by caring about them, by believing that they were worthy of help. When we are truly interested in people, we recognize their dignity and confirm our own by saying that we are all worthy of respect. There is dignity in simple labour to provide necessities and comforts for our families. There is none in the frantic accumulation of things. I know of no way to accumulate material wealth without abusing other people along the way. There is dignity in wanting to preserve a world in which the morning air smells sweet and the water is pure and the earth can feed us. There is no dignity in a way of life that finds arms production profitable and leaves us helplessly watching the trees die.

There is dignity in believing that we contain the stuff to be better than our destructive behaviour suggests. There is no dignity in wringing our hands over what a sad lot we are and deploring the selfishness and greed of human nature. I think we had better not count on a new messiah coming to make us all into the good people we can be.

I think it is up to us to believe that we are worth the effort to survive well.

That sounds like dignity to me.

In his "Viewpoint" of April 12, 2006, Allan Dennis, former editor of *Almaguin News* (*Almaguin Publishing* (1989) Limited) wrote, "After 18 years, the space on the other side of his page that was filled weekly by the wonderful words of Richard Thomas will now see a group of 12 take over. Each week one of the 12 people will contribute a column under the heading of 'Guest Column.' We begin the series this week with Richard's daughter Sarah contributing her talent…. Of course, we will never replace the style or talent of Richard Thomas. His contribution was one of a kind."

Notes

Foreword

1. Everett Kirton, *Logging Days in Parry Sound District* (Powassan, ON: self-published, 1977) 31. Property of Nipissing Museum, used with permission.

Introduction

1. Argyle Community Library, Mc*Conkey Corners* (Port Loring, ON: Canadore College North Bay, 1983), np.
2. *Almaguin News* (Almaguin Publishing (1989) Ltd), July 24, 1996.
3. Everett Kirton, *History of Northern Parry Sound District* (Powassan, ON: self-published, 1962) Introduction. Property of Nipissing Museum.
4. *Burk's Falls Arrow and Sundridge Echo*, July 6, 1966.
5. Rev. John S. Firmin, *Other Places, Parry Sound District, Spence, Chapman, Armour, Ryerson and Strong Townships* (self-published, 1977), np.
6. *Almaguin News* (Almaguin Publishing (1989) Ltd), July 10, 1996.
7. *McConkey Corners*, 1983, np.
8. Ibid.
9. Government of Canada website: www.parl.gc.ca/common.index.asp, accessed on August 20, 2006.
10. North Simcoe Hospital Alliance website: www.nsha.on.ca/history.htm, accessed on August 20, 2006.
11. *Almaguin News*, August 24, 1996.
12. A.T. "Dob" Walton and W.W. Walton, *The Steamer Kawigamog* (Powassan, ON: self-published, 1991) 10.
13. Kirton, *Logging Days in Parry Sound District*, 36.

Notes

Chapter One: A Settler's Story: The Founding of Burk's Falls

1. Thomas McMurray, *The Free Grant Lands of Canada from Practical Experience of Bush Farming in the Free Grant Districts of Muskoka and Parry Sound* (Bracebridge, ON: Northern Advocate, 1871), 103. Second edition by Fox Meadow Creations and Brad Hammond, Huntsville, Ontario, 2002.
2. *Toronto Mail*, July 30, 1892.
3. *Up the Muskoka and Down the Trent, Muskoka and Haliburton, 1615–1875, a Collection of Documents*, (*Toronto Globe, October 4, 1865*) Ontario Series of the Champlain Society for the Government of Ontario, obtained from Florence B. Murray.
4. Thomas McMurray, *The Free Grant Lands of Canada...*, 50, 116, 140.
5. Ibid, 117.
6. *Toronto Mail*, July 30, 1892.
7. Thomas McMurray, *The Free Grant Lands of Canada...*, 104.
8. Ibid, 104,105.
9. *Toronto Mail*, July 30, 1892.
10. *Toronto Globe*, October 4, 1865.
11. Larry Barry (ed.) *Memories of Burk's Falls and District: Village of Burk's Falls*, (published by the Village of Burk's Falls, 1978), 8.
12. *Oshawa Times*, November 3, 1984.
13. *Almaguin News*, July 7, 1976.
14. *Toronto Mail*, July 30, 1892.
15. Larry Barry (ed.), *Memories of Burk's Falls and District: Village of Burk's Falls*, 91.
16. *Toronto Mail*, July 30, 1892.
17. Larry Barry (ed.), *Memories of Burk's Falls and District: Village of Burk's Falls*, 95.
18. *Burk's Falls Arrow*, May 2, 1890.
19. Larry Barry (ed.), *Memories of Burk's Falls and District: Village of Burk's Fall*, 8.
20. *Oshawa Times*, November 3, 1984.

Chapter Two: Pioneer Adventures: The Arrival of the Train

1. Thomas McMurray, *The Free Grant Lands of Canada...* , 50.
2. Letters of Dr. Howard Anderson, 1967, Sundridge, Strong Union Public Library Archives.
3. From the files of Howard Watson Anderson, Sundridge, Strong Union Public Library Archives.
4. *North Bay Nugget*, September 3, 1974.
5. *Almaguin News* (Almaguin Publishing (1989) Limited), September 3, 1971.
6. Letters of Emma Anderson, April 2, 1967, Sundridge, Strong Union Public Library Archives.

7. *Toronto Mail*, July 30, 1892.
8. Larry Barry (ed.), *Memories of Burk's Falls and District* (Village of Burk's Falls, 1978), 8.
9. Rev. J. Macartney, *Historical Sketch of Sundridge* (self-published, 1946), the Sundridge Strong Union Public Library Archives.
10. Letters of Dr. Howard Anderson, 1967.
11. Rev. J. Macartney, *Historical Sketch of Sundridge*.
12. Notes of Merrill Dunbar at Sundridge, Strong Union Public Library Archives.
13. Patricia Lee, Alice May Robins (ed.), *The Lake in the Hills, Strong Township and Sundridge, 1875-1925* (Colbalt, ON: Highway Book Store, 1989), 5.
14. Letters of Dr. Howard Anderson, 1967.
15. Ibid.
16. Letters of Emma Anderson, not dated.
17. Letters of Dr. Howard Anderson.
18. *Toronto Mail*, July 9, 1892.
19. Letter from John Milne's great-grandson Doug Cox, dated October 27, 1994, obtained from Doug Cox.
20. Patricia Lee, Alice May Robins (ed.), *The Lake in the Hills, Strong Township and Sundridge, 1875–1925*, 52.
21. Letters of Jack Milne to Dr. Howard Anderson, June 23, 1955, at Sundridge, Strong Union Public Library Archives.
22. Ibid.
23. Ibid.
24. *Almaguin News* (Almaguin Publishing (1989) Limited), September, 1971.
25. "A Klondike Adventure" as told by John L. Anderson in 1953, notes and letters held at the Sundridge, Strong Union Public Library Archives.
26. Ibid.
27. Letters of Howard Anderson, undated.
28. Klondike History www.touryukon.com/Goldrush.asp, accessed on May 20, 2006.
29. Clipping from a Vancouver daily newspaper containing family information, undated, sent to the Andersons in Sundridge, by family members in living in Vancouver.
30. *Almaguin News* (Almaguin Publishing (1989) Limited), September 1971.

Chapter Three: The Life of a River Driver

1. *In Celebration of the Old Nipissing Road. 1875–2000* (A Magnetawan Millennium Group Project, 2000), 96.
2. Ibid, 94.
3. *Burk's Falls Arrow and Sundridge Echo*, July 6, 1966.
4. C. Gunning, *North Bay's Start Point 1882*: Early Arrivals Tell Their Own Stories (North Bay, ON: self-published, 1998), np.

5. *Burk's Falls Arrow and Sundridge Echo,* May 10, 1951.
6. *In Celebration of the Old Nipissing Road, 1875–2000,* 96.
7. Ibid, 62.
8. Ibid.

Chapter Four: A Century of Child Care in the Parry Sound District

1. Vera King, Memories of Children in the Care of the Parry Sound Children's Aid Society (Nipissing-Parry Sound CAS, May 2001), np.
2. *Burk's Falls Arrow,* September 20, 1917.
3. Lynda Elmy (ed.) *Animaltalk,* Fall/Winter 2006, 14.
4. Ibid.
5. Perry Township Agricultural Society minutes, April 28, 1917.
6. Ibid, January 19, 1918.
7. Tweedsmuire Village History, Book 1. Emsdale-Scotia Women's Institute, np.
8. *McConkey Corners,* 1983, np.
9. Ibid.
10. Interview with Dob Walton, reprinted in *Almaguin News,* August 14, 1996.
11. *McConkey Corners,* 1983, np.
12. *Burk's Falls Arrow,* July 1937.
13. *McConkey Corners,* 1983, np.
14. Ibid.
15. Dr. M.A. Wittick (as told to Helen Maddeaux), *The Doctor Who Never Refused a Call* (Sprucedale, ON: self-published, 1977), np.
16. Larry J. Barry (ed.), *Memories of Burk's Falls and District 1835–1978* (Village of Burk's Falls), 84.
17. Evelyn Howell (ed.), *Reflections of A Century Burk's Falls 1890–1990* (Village of Burk's Falls, 1990), 11.
18. Larry Barry (ed.), *Memories of Burk's Falls and District 1835–1978,* 95.
19. Larry Barry (ed.), *Memories of Burk's Falls and District 1835–1978,* 95; Evelyn Howell (ed.), *Reflections of A Century Burk's Falls 1890–1990,* 20.

Chapter Five: The South River Connection

1. Everett Kirton, *History of Northern Parry Sound District* (Powassan, ON: self-published, 1962) 23, 24. Property of Nipissing Museum.
2. *Almaguin News* (Almaguin Publishing (1989) Limited), August 7, 1974.
3. Everett Kirton, *History of Northern Parry Sound District,* 26.
4. Ibid, 23.
5. *Almaguin News* (Almaguin Publishing (1989) Limited), August 7, 1974.

6. E. Kirton, *History of Northern Parry Sound District*, 22.
7. Ibid, 26.
8. Everett Kirton, *History of Northern Parry Sound District*, 22,23.
9. Ibid, 23.
10. Ibid, 24.
11. Everett Kirton, *Logging Days in Parry Sound District*, 24.
12. Everett Kirton, *History of Northern Parry Sound District*, 26.
13. Family letters of Mrs. Eva MacIntosh, South River, July 14, 2000, files from Doug Mackay, Feb. 22, 2002.
14. Ibid.
15. *Near North Sun*, July 18, 1985.
16. *Family letters of Mrs. Eva MacIntosh*.
17. *Highland Herald*, February 9, 1988.
18. Family letters of Mrs. Eva MacIntosh.
19. Archival files, South River-Machar Union Public Library.
20. Information taken from notes provided from Art Loney, Doug Mackay and Gail Maeck.
21. Family letters of Mrs. Eva MacIntosh.
22. Ibid.
23. Archival files, South River-Machar Union Public Library.
24. *Almaguin News* (Almaguin Publishing (1989) Limited), August 7, 1974.
25. Archival files, South River-Machar Union Public Library.
26. *Near North Sun*, July 18, 1985.

Chapter Six: Arthur G. Peuchen: A Survivor

1. Margaret "Molly" Tobin Brown, an American socialite who eventually became an influential philanthropist, was actually the daughter of Irish immigrants. In the spring of 1912, her European tour cut short because of a family emergency back in America, she booked first-class passage on the *Titanic*. When the ship hit an iceberg and began to sink, Margaret proved to be instrumental in quieting the panic-stricken people aboard Lifeboat 6. Upon rescue she was quoted as saying she survived due to "typical Brown luck...we're unsinkable." From that moment on she became known as the "unsinkable Molly Brown."
2. John Hugo Ross, the son of Arthur Wellington Ross, was born in Toronto on November 25, 1875. The family moved to Winnipeg shortly afterwards in June 1877. Although he attended schools in both Vancouver and Toronto, he returned to Winnipeg in 1894 and began building his fortune. He founded the Hugo Ross Realty Company Ltd. and was also the president of both the Winnipeg Real Estate Exchange and Ross-MacMillan-Knight, a general insurance agency for Western Canada. He was just thirty-six years of age when he died aboard the *Titanic*. Brief biography prepared from notes

compiled by the Manitoba Library Association for the publication of *Pioneers and Early Citizens of Manitoba*, published in 1971. Encyclopedia Titanica, www.encyclopedia-titanica.org/biography/234/, accessed on Nov. 17 and Dec. 5, 2006.

3. Hichens's performance was that of a man described as "scared to death." He made a number of "wrong calls." Yet he was the person in charge of the lifeboat.
4. From *The Sunday Sun*, April 13, 1986, Encyclopedia Titanica www.encyclopedia-titanica.org/biography/234/, accessed on November 17 and December 5, 2006.

Chapter Seven: Pickerel River Logging Days

1. Everett Kirton, *Logging Days in Parry Sound District*, 3.
2. For more on the Ontario Lumber Company and the early French River settlement, see Wayne Kelly, *Capturing the French River: Images Along One of Canada's Most Famous Waterways, 1910–1927*. Toronto: A Natural Heritage Book/The Dundurn Press, 2007.
3. Article by John Macfie, *Parry Sound North Star*, June 30, 2004.
4. Everett Kirton, *Logging Days in Parry Sound District*, 3.
5. David Mclaren, *Turn of the Century Stories About Northern Pioneers from the Early 1900s* (Cobalt, ON: Highway Book Shop, 1992), 1.
6. The Victoria Harbour Lumber Company was founded by John Waldie who, at the time of his death in 1907, was identified as "the second largest lumber operator in Canada." For more information on Waldie and his company, see *The Legacy of John Waldie and Sons: A History of the Victoria Lumber Company*. Toronto: A Natural Heritage Book/The Dundurn Press, 2007.
7. Everett Kirton, *Logging Days in Parry Sound District*, 3.
8. *McConkey Corners*, 1983.
9. *Almaguin News*, October 1, 1975
10. Everett Kirton, *Logging Days in Parry Sound District*, 4.
11. *Almaguin News*, October 1, 1975.
12. Everett Kirton, *Logging Days in Parry Sound District*, 4.
13. *McConkey Corners*, 1983.
14. Everett Kirton, *Logging Days in Parry Sound District*, 11.
15. *McConkey Corners*, 1983.
16. Everett Kirton, *History of Northern Parry Sound District*, 3.
17. Government of Canada website www.parl.gc.ca/common.index.asp, accessed on August 20, 2006)
18. *McConkey Corners*, 1983.
19. Ibid.
20. John Macfie, *Up the Great North Road: The Story of an Ontario Colonization Road* (Erin, ON: Boston Mills Press, 2004), 67.
21. *McConkey Corners*, 1983.

22. Ibid.
23. John Macfie, *Up the Great North Road: The Story of an Ontario Colonization Road*, 67.
24. *McConkey Corners*, 1983.
25. Ibid.
26. Ibid.
27. John Macfie, *Parry Sound North Star*, February 23, 2005.
28. Everett Kirton, *Logging Days in Parry Sound District*, 3.

Chapter Eight: Lost Channel: A Company Town

1. Everett Kirton, *Logging Days in Parry Sound District*, 11.
2. *McConkey Corners*, 1983.
3. Toronto's Past www.brucebelltours.com/html/Toronto_s_past.html, accessed on September 20, 2006.
4. *McConkey Corners*, 1983.
5. Ibid.
6. Everett Kirton, *Logging Days in Parry Sound District*, 12.
7. Ibid, 32.
8. *McConkey Corners*, 1983.
9. Ibid.
10. Everett Kirton, *Logging Days in Parry Sound District*, 3.
11. Ibid, 17.
12. Everett Kirton, *Logging Days in Parry Sound District*, 12.
13. Ibid, 36.
14. Ibid, 34.
15. *McConkey Corners*, 1983.
16. Ibid.
17. Everett Kirton, *Logging Days in Parry Sound District*, 34.
18. *McConkey Corners*, 1983.
19. Everett Kirton, *Logging Days in Parry Sound District*, 35.
20. Ibid.
21. *McConkey Corners*, 1983.
22. Ibid.
23. Everett Kirton, *Logging Days in Parry Sound District*, 36.
24. *Almaguin News*, August 14, 1996.
25. Everett Kirton, *Logging Days in Parry Sound District*, 2.
26. John Macfie, *Parry Sound North Star*, June 30, 2004.
27. Everett Kirton, *Logging Days in Parry Sound District*, 12.
28. Alan Bell, *A Way West: A Canadian Railway Legend* (Barrie, ON: self-published, 1991), 60.

Chapter Nine: The Last Stands

1. Everett Kirton, *Logging Days in Parry Sound District*, 24.
2. Ibid.
3. Ibid, 36.
4. Ibid.
4. *McConkey Corners*, 1983.
5. Ibid.
6. Ibid.
7. Ibid.
8. Everett Kirton, *Logging Days in Parry Sound District*, 12.
9. *McConkey Corners*, 1983.
10. Ibid.
11. Everett Kirton, *Logging Days in Parry Sound District*, 12, 13.
12. Ibid, 38.
13. *McConkey Corners*, 1983.

Chapter Ten: The Walton Family: Boat Builders

1. *McConkey Corners*, 1983.
2. *Almaguin News*, August 14, 1996; A.T. "Dob" Walton and W.W. Walton, *The Steamer Kawigamog* (Powassan, ON: self-published, 1991), 1.
3. *McConkey Corners*, 1983.
4. Ibid.
5. *Almaguin News*, July 17, 1996.
6. Ibid.
7. Walton and Walton, *The Steamer Kawigamog*, 4.
8. *Almaguin News*, July 17, 1996.
9. Walton and Walton, *The Steamer Kawigamog*, 7.
10. *Almaguin News*, July 31, 1966.
11. Everett Kirton, *Logging Days in Parry Sound District*, 36.
12. *McConkey Corners*, 1983.
13. *Almaguin News*, August 14, 1996.
14. Ibid, July 31, 1996.
15. *Almaguin News*, July 17, 1996.
16. Ibid.
17. *Almaguin News*, July 24, 1996.
18.. Ibid, July 17, 1996.
19. Ibid, August 24, 2004.
20. Ibid, July 24, 1996.

21. Everett Kirton, *Logging Days in Parry Sound District*, 37.
22. *Almaguin News*, August 14, 1996.
23. Ibid, July 24, 1996.
24. Ibid, July 17, 1996.
25. Walton and Walton, *Steamer Kawigamog*, 21.
26. Ibid, 26.

Chapter Eleven: A Life Remembered: Richard Thomas (1932–2006)

1. Information from files of the *Almaguin News* (Almaguin Publishing (1989) Limited), January 4, 2006; April 5, 2006; April, 12, 2006; *The Globe and Mail* and *Toronto Star*, April 8, 2006.

Chapter Twelve: A Boy Scout's Journey and Lake Cecebe's Bay

1. Information from files from Elwood Addison, *Burk's Falls Arrow* and from the *Almaguin News* (Almaguin Publishing (1989) Ltd).

Chapter Thirteen: Kearney: Home of Ontario Baseball Champions

1. From interviews with the McConkey family and municipal staff of the Town of Kearney, on June 3 and June 4, 2006).

Chapter Fourteen: Sundridge and the Johnstone Story

1. From the files of *Almaguin News* (Almaguin Publishing (1989) Limited), Johnstone family history provided by Lucy Rennie, and from interviews with the Johnstone family, over an extended period of time beginning in 2000.

Chapter Fifteen: The Bridge That Will Stand Forever

1. *Cawthra Scrapbooks*, private collection of Jane Gavine.

Appendix A: Poems and Songs of Clarence Brazier

1. The "Sweder" Mills Pine that Clarence Brazier refers to is the Schroeder Mills and Timber Company of Wisconsin. The company's cutting operation on the Key Valley River (Pickerel River) lasted from 1918 to 1923, just when Clarence was beginning to work in the lumber industry.
2. The "Town of Spence" reference is to the Township of Spence, now part of Magnetawan.

Appendix B: Trouble on the Tote Road by Everett Kirton

1. Taken from Everett Kirton, *Logging Days in Parry Sound District*, 15.

Bibliography

Barry, Larry (ed.), *Memories of Burk's Falls and District,* Village of Burk's Falls, 1978.

Bell. Alan, *A Way West, A Canadian Railway Legend.* Barrie, ON: self-published, 1991.

Firman, Rev. John S., *Other Places, Parry Sound District: Spence, Chapman, Armour, Ryerson and Strong Townships,* self-published, c.1977.

Gunning, C., *North Bay's Start Point 1882: Early Arrivals Tell Their Own Stories.* North Bay, ON: self-published, 1998.

Howell, Evelyn (ed.), *Reflections of A Century Burk's Falls 1890–1990.* Village of Burk's Falls, 1990.

In Celebration of the Old Nipissing Road, 1875–2000. A Magnetawan Millennium Group Project, 2000.

King, Vera, *Memories of Children in the Care of the Parry Sound Children's Aid Society.* Nipissing-Parry Sound CAS, 2001.

Kirton, Everett, *History of Northern Parry Sound District.* Powassan, ON: self-published, 1962.

_____, *Logging Days in Parry Sound District.* Powasson, ON: self-published, 1977. Property of Nipissing Museum.

Lee, Patricia, Alice May Robbins (ed.), *The Lake in the Hills, Strong Township and Sundridge, 1875–1925.* Colbalt, ON: Highway Book Store, 1989.

Macfie, John, *Up the Great North Road: The Story of an Ontario Colonization Road,* Erin, ON: Boston Mills Press, 2004.

McConkey Corners. Port Loring, ON: Argyle Community Library, 1983.

McMurray, Thomas, *The Free Grant Lands of Canada from Practical Experience of Bush Farming in the Free Grant Districts of Muskoka and Parry Sound.* Bracebridge, ON:, Northern Advocate, 1871. Second edition by Fox Meadows Creations and Brad Hammond, Huntsville, Ontario, 2002.

Tweedsmuire Village History, Book 1. Emsdale-Scotia Women's Institute. not paginated.

Up the Muskoka and Down the Trent Muskoka and Haliburton, 1615–1875: A Collection of

Documents (Toronto Globe, October 4, 1865), Ontario Series of the Champlain Society for the Government of Ontario, obtained from Florence B. Murray.

Walton, A.T. and W.W. Walton, *The Steamer Kawigamog*. Powasson, ON.: self-published, 1991.

Index

A.E. Ballard Meat Store (South River), 63
Adanac, 109
Addison:
    Bonnie (Walker) (Mrs. Elwood), 129
    Edwin, 122, 123, 126
    Elwood "Addie," 121–126, 128–132
Agar, Albert "Bert" A., 44, 45
Agar family, 124
Ahmic Harbour (ON), 15, 25, 26, 44, 46
Algonquin Park, 46, 60, 65, 70, 73, 115, 134, 150, 151, 162
Algonquin West Credit Union, 161
All Saints' Anglican Church (Burk's Falls), 52
Almaguin Highlands, 13, 40, 61, 102–104, 139, 150, 151
Almaguin News, 13, 111, 114, 115, 119, 121, 150, 162, 163
American Lumber Company, 77
Anderson:
    Emma Louise, 32, 33, 36–40
    Albert, 38
    William Edward, 38, 39
    Howard, 34, 36–39
    John, 38, 39
    Margaret (Milne) (Mrs. William), 33, 36
    Mary, see Mary Carter
    William, 33–36, 38

Anderson, Bert, 65, 67, 71
Anderson, Earl, 151
Arcan Company, 73
Archie Menzies Landing, 35
Ard, W.J., 64
Argus Corporation, 73
Armour (steamer), 15, 26, 31
Armour Township (Parry Sound District), 113, 119, 161
Armstrong, Alan, 127
Armstrong, __ (Dr.), 147
Armstrong, John, 87
Armstrong, __ (Sheriff), 147
Armstrong Boarding House (Burk's Falls), 17, 56
Armstrong Bridge, 147
Arnstein (ON), 55, 79, 99, 109
Arrow Press (Burk's Falls), 52, 57
Arthur, Andrew, 81
Arthur, Robert, 81
Arthur L. (steamer), 106
Atwell, Bob, 146
Atwell, Ron, 146
Austin, __ (Miss), 55
Avery, Margaret, see Margaret Kirton

Bagshaw, __ (Mr.), 36

Bailey, __ (Miss), 56
Ballantyne Township (Parry Sound District), 65
Barber (Bowmanville) Creek
Barlow, E., 137
Bartlett, B., 73
Barrie (ON), 115
Battalion, 162nd, 143, 148
Baxter, Len, 72, 73
Beale, __(Dr.), 105
Beatty Station, 97
Bell, Harvey S., 137
Bell, Jim (Dr.), 131
Belmore (ON), 33, 34, 36
Bernard Creek, 36
Berton, Jack, 67
Best, Sam, 2, 13, 103
Bice, Ralph, 162
Big Deer Lake, 92
Blackmoor Bay, 105
Blackmoor's Mill, 105
Blair Township (Parry Sound District), 92, 98
Blind Channel (BC), 39
Blind River (ON), 89
Bloomfield United Church, 143
Bolton, Eddie, 131
Booth, Eldon, 122
Booth, John Rudolphus "J.R.," 16, 61–63, 97
Boudreau:
    Angela, see Angela Brazier
    Armand, 46, 49
    Aurele, 46
    Joe, 46
    Regina (Mrs. Victor), 49
    Victor, 49
Bowers, Edgar, 106
Bowmanville (ON), 31
Boyd, Hannah (Kirton), 83, 84

Boyd, James, 83, 84
Boyes and Sons Construction Ltd. (Burk's Falls), 54
Bracebridge (ON), 22, 34, 38, 41, 79
Bradford (ON), 57
Bradford, Murray, 123
Brampton (ON), 143
Brantford (ON), 24, 41
Brasher, Fred, 27
Brazier:
    Angela (Boudreau) (Mrs. Clarence), 49
    Clarence, 13, 40–51, 152–158
    Donald, 41, 43
    Doris, see Doris Villemaire
    Earl, 41, 42, 45, 49
    Ethel, 41, 43, 46
    Frances Mae (Ward) (Mrs. George), 41, 43, 45, 48, 49
    George, 40–42, 44, 49
    Irene, 50
    Janet, 50
    Johnny, 41, 43, 45
    Pearl, 50
    Ron, 50
    Wallace, 41, 42
    William "Bill," 41, 43
Brear, Gordon, 128
Brook, Robert George, 16
Brook, Mary Lucy (Davis), 16
Brooks, Les, 71
Brooks, Robert, 102, 109
Brooks, Ted, 71
Brooks, William, 106
Brown, Doug "Samwyz," 129
Brown, Josephine (Mrs. Percy), 56
Brown, Mary-Kate, 130, 131
Brown, Margaret "Molly" (Mrs.), 74, 168
Brown, Percy, 56
Brown Township (Parry Sound District), 92
Brown's Boarding House (Burk's Falls), 56

Bruce, George, 17, 19, 98, 100
Bruce and Kirk Lumber Co., 98, 100, 107, 108
Bruce's Bay, 98
Brunne, Albert, 98, 99
Brunne's Apiary, 109
Brunne's Sawmill, 101
Bunt, Ted, 122, 128
Burch, Hilda (Miss), 56
Burk:
    Alice "Olive" (Simpson) (Mrs. Frank), 23, 27, 30
    David Sr., 22
    David Francis "Frank," 22–25, 27, 30, 57
    Francis, 30
    Ida, see Ida Johnson
    John, 30, 31
    Mabel, see Mabel Hendrichson
    Walter, 24, 27
Burk House, 24, 25, 27, 29, 30, 54
Burk's Falls (ON), 13–15, 24, 25, 27–30, 34, 37, 38, 41, 44, 46, 52, 5458, 71, 75, 83, 89, 111, 113, 116, 120, 123, 124, 127, 132, 147–49, 161
Burk's Falls, Armour, Ryerson Arena, 120
Burk's Falls Arrow, 52, 53, 121, 122, 126, 147, 150, 151
Burk's Falls Cemetery, 27
Burk's Falls Cubs, 122
Burk's Falls Girl Guides, 126, 127
Burk's Falls Lions Club, 121, 126–30
Burk's Falls Scout Troup, 1st, 121, 122, 124, 126, 127, 131, 132
Burk's Falls Shelter, 52, 53
Burk's Falls Tannery houses, 41
Burnsides, A., 140
Bush, Tommy, 67
Byng Inlet, 78, 79, 91
Byrnes, Charles, 62
Byrnes, Joan, 139
Byrnes, Paul, 139

Cain, Bridget, 16
Cain, Joe, 55
Cain, Kate, 16
Cain, Maggie, 16
Cain, Mary (Mrs. Joe), 55
Callander (ON), 62
Cameron, Crystal, see Crystal LaBrash
Campbell, __ (Dr.), 82
Campbell, Algie, 143
Campbell, Dale, 143
Campbell, Jane Anne "Jenny," see Jane Anne Thomas
Canadian National Railway (CNR), 11, 105
Canadian Pacific Railway (CPR), 19, 94, 99, 100, 109
Canada Pine Lumber Company, 46, 154
Carey, George, 92
Caribou Creek, 98
Caribou Lake, 16
Carter:
    Effie, 36
    John, 32, 36, 38, 39
    Mary (Anderson), 32, 36, 38
Carter, Robert, 62
Carter family, 140, 141,
Cataract House (Burk's Falls), 29, 56
Cawthra, Dave, 75
Cawthra, George, 75
Chaffey Township (Muskoka District), 25
Chapman, W.H. (watchmaker), 63
Chapman Township (Parry Sound District), 49
Charlebois:
    Andre, 93
    Bernadette, 93
    Pauline, 93
Chaudière Dam, 98
Chemmens, Ross, 65, 67, 71

Chew, Manley, 16, 17
Chew brothers, 16, 17
Children's Aid Society (CAS), 53, 54, 58
Children's Aid Society (Parry Sound), 52, 56
Children's Aid Society, 53, 54
Chrétien, Jean (Prime Minister), 119
Christie Township (Parry Sound District), 97
Clapperton, 110
Clapperton, Bill, 16
Clapperton, Florence, 16
Clapperton, Oscar, 109
Clark, Eliza Eleanor, see Eliza Peuchen
Clark, George, 57
Clee, __ (Dr.), 95, 109
Clifton House (Burk's Falls), 25, 27, 28, 30
Cole's Mill, 89, 105
Colorado Avalanche, 146
Comfort, Jean (Thomas), 113
Coniston Smelter, 49
Conn, Earl, 67
Cook, Edward (Private), 75
Cook, Herman H., 77
Cook, Guy, 95
Cook, Lydia (Mrs. H.H.), 77
Cook, Robert, 106
Cooper, Frank "A.F.," 65–67
Cooper, Orlo (Orly), 65, 67, 68, 71
Copps, Sheila, 117
Corkery Falls Dam, 61
Craig, Ernie, 137
Cripps, Bill, 122, 126
Cripps, Cliff, 122
Croft Township (Parry Sound District), 40
Croswell, Dora, 82
Croswell, William, 82
Crozier, William, 99
Culbert, Doug, 123
Culbert, Ron, 123
Currie, John and Annie, 84
Currie, Johnston, 81, 84

Cyclone (steamer), 44

Daisy, 110
Danube (steamer), 39
Darling, Stan (MP), 25, 127
Darlington Generating Station, 31
Darlington Provincial Park, 31
Darlington Township (Ontario County), 30
Davis, Henry, 55
Davis, Jim "Pop," 105, 106, 108
Davis, Martha, 105
Davis, Michael James, 83
Davis, Sarah (Kirton) (Mrs. M.J.), 83
Davis' Point, 83
Day House (Burk's Falls), 57
Deer Lake, 78, 110
Dempster, T.C., 28
Dennis, Allan, 115, 119, 163
Dennis, Stuart, 151
Detroit (MI), 19
Detroit Red Wings, 146
deVries, Greg, 146
Dickie, Joe, 49
Dingman, Rick, 129
Dixon, Oliver, 96
Dobbs family, 82
Doe Bay, 34
Doe Lake, now Whalley Lake, 40
Doherty, Everett, 126, 130, 132
Dokis Reserve, 98
Dollar, John Melville, 19, 77
Dollar, Walter, 19
Dollars Dam, 20, 86, 104, 105, 109
Dollars Lake, 19, 79, 87, 89, 108
Dominion Tar and Chemical (Montreal), 73
Douglas, James, 57
Douglas L. (steamer), 106
Drew, __ (Capt.), 111
Duck Lake, 12, 104, 105, 107–109
Dumble, Minnie (Miss), 53

Dunbar, Bertha, 141
Dunbar, James, 35
Dunchurch (ON), 79, 81–83, 150

Eagle Lake, 62, 63
East Parry Sound CAS, 53, 55, 58, 59
Edgar, Mary S., 33
Edgar, Joseph, 38
Edgington Station, 97
Edmonton (AB), 115
Elias Rogers Coal and Lumber Company (Toronto), 89
Elora (ON), 33
Emerson, Mary (Mrs. Joseph), 128, 129
Empey, Arthur L., 98, 106
Empey Lumber Company, 106, 108
Emsdale (ON), 55, 119, 135, 151
Emulator (steamer), 2, 13, 103
English, Fred, 142
English Trader, 76
Ennis, Daniel, 16
Ennis, Florence, 93
Ennis, John, 16, 93
Erb, William, 62
Ethel (ON), 34–36
Everest, Bob, 67
Eves, Ernie (Premier), 117–119

Fagan, Barney, 81, 84
Fairview Hotel/Red Hotel, 16
Fairy Lake, 34
Falconbridge Baseball Team, 137
Faulkner, J.C., 139
Fell, John, 122, 127
Fergus (ON), 33
Ferrie Township (Parry Sound District), 81, 82
First World War (Great War), 11, 16, 64, 75, 76, 86, 95, 143, 149
Flannigan's Landing, 142
Fleming, Fred, 16

Fleming house, 105
Flynn, Jim, 35
Flynn, Pat, 35
Follick, Don, 31
Forsyth, Ed "Eddie," 14, 105
Forsyth, Edmund Sr., 82
Foster, Thomas, 77
Fowler, Harvey, 128, 130
French, __ (Mr.), 141
French River, 77, 87, 98
Fraser, John, 61, 80
Fraser Lumber Co., 61, 80
Frost, Walter, 67
Furlong, George, 67

Galna, John (MPP). 147, 148
Galna Bridge, 147, 148
Georgian Bay, 19, 21, 77, 78, 87, 90, 92, 150, 151
Georgian Bay Lumber Co., 98
Gibson, Al, 123
Glen Bernard Camp (Sundridge), 33
Glen Rosa, also Glenrosa (steamer), 2, 13, 25, 103
Glenada (steamer), 13, 14
Glenila (ON), 79, 81, 83
Glenny family, 28
Glover, __ (Mr.), 36
Glover family, 43
Gogama (ON), 46
Golden Valley (ON), 16, 55, 82, 90, 98
Gorham:
    Minnie Delphine, see Minnie Kirton
    Sarah Ann (Coon), 84
    Thomas Jasper, 84
Gould, Brock, 131
Goulding, Sam, 123, 126
Government of Ontario
    Department of Lands and Forests, 12, 85, 100

Graham, Don, 123, 126
Grand Trunk Railway, 11, 32, 54, 62, 63, 73, 149
Grant and Dunn Lumber Co., 46
Gravenhurst (ON), 11, 32, 34, 38, 57, 79
Gravenhurst (steamer), 31
Graves and Bigwood Lumber Co., 78, 79, 92
Great Depression, 49, 56, 67, 68, 123, 137147
Green Bay, 124, 128–130
Green Bay Scout Camp, 121, 125, 129, 132
Guthrie, Johnny, 16
Guthrie, Tom, 16

H.W. Trimmer House (Burk's Falls), 28
Haggart, Harky, 109
Haggart, Janet Ann (Robertson) (Mrs. John), 81
Haggart, Jean, 55
Haggart, John, 81
Haldimand, County of, 83
Haliburton, District of, 71, 89
Hall, Sarah (Miss), 143
Hall, Ray, 142
Hall, Ron. 151
Hamilton (ON), 11, 130
Hampel, Fred, 95
Hannell, Frederick, 77
Hanson, G.F. "Rusty," 72
Harcourt (ON), 71
Harcourt, ___ (Dr.), 16
Harden, Alf, 124, 125
Hardy, Katie (Buchanan), 140
Hardy Lumber Co., 79
Hardy Township (Parry Sound District), 79, 80, 92, 98
Harkness, Harkie, 94
Harrison, Ada, 49
Harrison, Bill, 49

Hartill, John, 52–56
Hassard, Sarah, see Sarah McConkey
Hay & Company (Woodstock), 24, 73
Haywood, ___ (Miss), 55
Hendrichson, Mabel (Burk), 24, 30
Hendrichson, Richard, 30
Heritage River Walk (Burk's Falls), 149
Hettler Lumber Co., 98
Hichens, Florence Mortimer, 76
Hichens, (Hitchens) Robert, 75
Hicks, Thomas, 49
Hilliar
    Horace Knight, 57
    Joseph Frederick, 57, 59, 123, 124
    Mary Nettie (Knight) (Mrs. J.F.), 53, 57
    William Underhill, 55, 57
Hilliar Hardware Store (Burk's Falls), 57
Hillis, Lila, 28
Hinton (AB), 76
Holland-Graves Lumber Co., 78, 79
Holt, Bill, 67
Holt Timber Company, 92
Hooper, Bill, 73
Hope, Ted, 46
Horn Lake, 89
Hotel Central (Burk's Falls), 53
Howich Township (Huron County), 33
Howland, Lucien B., 89, 90, 96
Hubbert, Sarah, 130, 131
Hunter, Ab, 38
Hunter, Bill, 38
Hunter, Peter, 122
Hunter, Roddy, 123
Huntsville (ON), 22, 34, 36–38, 43, 66, 130
Huntsville Tannery, 66
Huron, County of, 33, 34, 36, 83

Independent Grocers Alliance (IGA), 139
Innes, Sutherland, 144
Irwin, Walter, 137

Irwin, Wilmot, 137
Iverson, Martin, 67

J.B. Smith Lumber Co., 98
J.R. Booth Lumber Co., 62
James, George, 67
Jamieson, __ (Dr.), 105
Jeffrey's Motor Company (Wisconsin), 37
Johnson, Ida (Burk), 30
Johnson, John, 30
Johnson, Pauline, 24
Johnston, Wilfred, 65, 67
Johnstone:
    Amanda "A.E." (Mundt) (Mrs. J.P.), 139–145
    Arlene (Mrs. Bob), 139
    Bob, 139, 144
    Dave, 139, 144
    Evelyn (Summers) (Mrs. Fred), 139, 145
    Fred, 139, 142, 144, 145
    Lucy, see Lucy Rennie
    John Philemon "J.P.," 139, 140, 142–145
    J.P. Jr., 142
    Pat (Mrs. Dave), 139
    Ross, 145
Johnstone's Bakery, 139, 141
Johnstone's Food Market (General Merchants), 139, 140, 145
Johnstone's Tourist Camp, 143–145
Jones, James, 62
Jordan, Wes, 137

Katrine (ON), 13, 23, 34, 131
Kam Kotia Road, 49
Kawigamog (steamer), 11–13, 102, 104, 105, 108–112
Kawigamog Lodge, 95
Kearney (ON), 46, 115, 119, 120, 134–138, 161, 162

Kearney Community Centre, 134
Kearney General Store, 120
Kearney House, 135
Kelcey:
    Edward, 82, 83
    George, 82
    Lily (Metcalfe) (Mrs. Edward), 82, 83
    Lucy Ann (Mannering), 82
Kelcey Lake, 78
Kelsey, __ (Capt.), 105
Kelso, John, 53–55
Kemp, George, 144
Kennedy, "Black" Jack, 87
Kennedy, Tom (Capt.), 111
Kenosha (WI), 37
Key Harbour, 85, 97
Key Lake, 89, 105
Key River, 85, 97
Key Valley, 11, 100
Key Valley Railway, 19, 84, 94, 96, 97, 99, 100
Kickham, __ (Dr.), 53
Kidd, Cecil T., 14, 101
Kidd's Landing, 17, 19, 78
Kidd's Home Hardware (Sundridge), 140
King:
    Annie (Wilson) (Mrs. Tom), 40
    John, 40
    Maria (Mrs. John), 40
    Tom, 40
Kitchener (ON), 62
Kirton:
    Carl, 85
    Elizabeth (Mrs. James), 83
    Elma (Ward) (Mrs. Everett), 12, 85
    Eva Lillian, 84
    Everett, 12, 13, 84–87, 89–94, 96, 98, 101, 159
    Francis Archie, 84
    Hannah, see Hannah Boyd

Henry, 81, 83
Ida Laurena, 84
Glenn, 85
James, 83
Jasper Earle, 84
John Lawrence, 84
Margaret (Avery) (Mrs. Henry), 83
Margaret May, 84
Mary, see Mary Wiley
Minnie Delphine (Gorham) (Mrs. William), 84, 85
Sarah, see Sarah Davis
William, 81, 83–85
William Jr., 84
Knight, Henry "Harry," 27
Knight, Moses, 57
Knight, Walter, 27
Knight Bros. Sash and Door Factory (Burk's Falls), 27, 59, 107
Kulchar, Nick, 131
Kyle, Johnny, 16
Kyle, William, 16

LaBarre, __ (Mr.), 128
LaBrash, Crystal (Mrs. James), 90, 95
Lady Isabella Nursing Home (Trout Creek), 57
Lady Katrine (steamer), 2, 13, 103
Laidlaw Lumber Company (Toronto), 65
Lake Bernard, 34, 39, 122, 124, 141, 143, 144
Lake Bernard Park, 122
Lake Cecebe, 14, 25, 124, 128
Lake Huron, 77
Lake Nipissing, 60–63
Lake Nosbonsing, 62
Lake Superior, 89
Lakeview Hotel, 109
Lamb, Ernie, 72
Lanark, County of, 27

Lane, Bill, 38, 39
Lang, Willard, 141
Lang, William, 36, 141
Lang's General Store, 38
Latchford (ON), 46
Lauder, James, 89, 96
Lauder, Spears and Howland Lumber Co., 89, 90, 92, 94, 96, 99
Laughlin:
    Bert, 93
    Edith, 93
    Gertie, see Gertie Rutherford
Laurier Township (Parry Sound District), 62–64
Layolomi Beach Inn, 39
Leal, H. Allan (Q.C.), 117
Lightoller, Charles Herbert (2nd Officer), 75
Livingstone, __ (Miss), 55
Loney, Art, 67, 68, 71, 73
Loney, Bill, 67
Longford Mills (Orillia), 65, 72
Long Island, New York
Long Lake, 99
Long Lake Lumber Co., 98
Loring (ON), 12, 14, 16, 20, 55, 56, 78–85, 87, 94, 108–110
Loring Cemetery, 83
Loring Deer Yard, 101
Lost Channel (ON), 11–13, 17, 19, 84, 86, 87, 89–101, 105, 107, 109–111
Lost Channel Blabber, 90
Ludgate:
    Douglas, 97
    James Sr., 97
    James, 96, 97, 106
Ludgate Lumber Company, 97
Lydiatt, Jeff, 65

MacDonald, "Bucko," 146
MacDonald, Frank E., 77

Machar Township (Parry Sound District), 62–64
MacIntosh, Jim, 67
MacKay, Murray, 130, 131
Maddeaux, Helen, 57
Maeck, Gail (Stringer), 70
Magnetawan (ON), 13, 26, 34, 40, 41, 55, 60, 102, 124, 127, 129, 131
Magnetawan, District of, 21
Magnetawan Central School, 42
Magnetawan Community Centre, 42
Magnetawan River, 11, 13–15, 20, 22–26, 30, 31, 34, 41, 44, 57, 78, 79, 91, 92, 97, 102, 104, 107, 128, 147, 150
Magentawan River and Lakes Steamboat Company, 30, 45, 150
Magnetawan River Railway Company, 27, 147
Magnetawan River Tannery Company, 17, 59
Magnetawan Seniors' Friendship Centre, 49
Maloney, Maurice, 108
Manley Chew Bros. (Midland), 92, 98
Mann, Bob, 136
Mannering, Lucy Ann, see Lucy Ann Kelcey
Manning, Ted, 109
Manning lot, 103
Maple Lake Station, 99
Mark, Dave W., 137
Marsden's Landing, 19, 44
Mary Lake, 34
Masonic Lodge (Burk's Falls), 59
Matthew's farm, 105
McAdams, __ (Mr.), 62
McCallum, Albert, 79
McCastle, Norman, 92
McConaghy, Albert, 72
McConkey:
    Chester, 134, 136, 137
    Janet (Mrs. Wilfred), 137
    Marion, 137
    Mary Ann, see Mary Ann Ross, 137
    Maxwell, 137
    Robert Jr., 134, 136, 137
    Robert Sr., 134, 136, 137
    Sarah (Hassard) (Mrs. R.Sr.), 134
    Susan, see Susan Roncadin
    Theresa Agnes (Mrs. Chester), 137
    Wilfred, 134, 136–138
McConkey Corners, 80, 81, 87
McConkey, Township of (Parry Sound District), 78–80, 82, 92, 98
McConnell, Bill, 17
McCormick and Irwin Lumber Co., 79
McCreary, Bill Jr., 146
McCreary, Bill Sr., 146
McCreary, Keith, 146
McDermott, Ben, 36
McDiarmid, __ (Miss), 55
McGibbon, __ (Miss), 65, 67
McGibbon Lumber Co. (Penetang), 92
McIndoo, Vic, 122
McIntyre Mine, 48
McIssac, Elsie, 65, 67
McKay, Murray, 126
McKellar (ON), 82
McKenzie, Township of (Parry Sound District), 78, 92
McLachlan, Jean, see Jean Partridge
McLaughton, K.S., 73
McLish, Dave, 67
McMillian family, 27
McMurchy, Alex, 143
McMurray, Thomas, 22
McMurrich, Township of, (Parry Sound District), 161
McNaughton, Ian, 131
McNaughton, "Mickey," 128
McVey, Beatrice (Mrs. Stan), 128, 129
Meaford (ON), 107

Mendelson Joe, 114
Menzies, Archie, 36
Menzies, Robert H., 57
Merriam, Pearl (Miss), 55
Messrss Shaw and Ryan (South River), 63
Metcalf, Arnold, 125
Metcalf, John, 123
Metcalfe, Lily, see Lily Kelcey
Methodist Point (Midland), 16
Michener, Roland (Gov. Gen.), 131
Midland (ON), 16, 17, 92, 98, 100
Midlothian Bridge, 15
Mike (tugboat), 107
Millen, William, 40
Miller, Andrew, 15
Miller, Derek, 132
Miller, Glenn, 131, 132
Miller, Norm (MPP), 132
Mills, Township of (Parry Sound District), 79, 80, 84, 92
Milne:
    Eliza (Mrs. John), 34, 37
    Jack, 37, 38
    James, 34, 36
    John Sr., 33
    John, 34–37
    Mary (Woir) (Mrs. John Sr.), 33, 36
    Walter, 37, 38
Milne's family, 45
Minden (ON), 41
Minorgan, Bob, 143
Mitchell, Margaret (Mrs. Frank), 128
Mitchell, Howard, 65, 67
Molten, Earl, 47, 48
Montreal (QC), 64, 72–74, 77, 96
Montreal River, 46
Moon, __ (Judge), 55
Moore, Myron, 122
Moore Lumber, 46
Moorhouse, E. (Rev.), 126

Mountjoy, Township of, 49
Mowat Station, 89, 90, 105, 106
Mowat, Township of (Parry Sound District), 78, 89
Mulherson Bros. Ltd., 29
Mundt, Amanda, see Amanda Johnstone
Murdoch, A.J., 72
Murdoch, Peter, 69
Muskoka, District of, 11, 21, 40, 151
Muskoka and Georgian Bay Navigation Company, 25
Muskoka Literacy Council, 51
Muskoka-Nipissing-Parry Sound Cattlemen's Association, 119

National Literacy Award, 50
Nellie Bly (tugboat), 107
Neville Park, Toronto
Newcombe, see Dunchurch
New York, State of, 30, 31
Nickerson, __ (Miss), 16
Nicklon, Jim, 67
Nipissing, District of, 151
Nipissing-Parry Sound Children's Aid Society (CAS), 52
Nipissing Passageway, 47
Nipissing Township Museum, 85
Nipissing Village (ON), 60
Norland (ON), 41
North Bay (ON), 11, 20, 22, 32, 37, 55, 56, 61–63, 151
North Bay Granite Club, 145
North Star Hotel (Magnetawan), 49
North Tea Lake, 70
Novar (ON), 151

O'Brien, William Edward (MP), 80
O'Neill, William "Bill," 136, 137
Ontario Free Grants & Homestead Act (1868), 21, 22, 34, 60, 82

Ontario Lumber Company (OLC), 19, 77–80, 87, 92
Ontario Northland Railway (ONR), 48
Orange Hall (Burk's Falls), 124
Orillia (ON), 36, 65, 72, 74
Oshawa (ON), 22
Ottawa (ON), 61, 62
Ottawa, Arnprior & Parry Sound Railway, 97

Paget, John, 35
Paget's farm, 143
Pakesley (ON), 19, 94, 96, 97, 99, 100
Pakesley Lumber Company, 100, 107, 108
Parolin, August, 80
Parolin, Eva, 80
Parolin, Ida, 80
Parry Sound (ON), 11, 22, 46, 52, 79, 85, 89, 95, 96, 111, 150
Parry Sound, District of, 11, 13, 16, 17, 21, 22, 27, 49, 60, 73, 79, 80, 85, 87, 97, 98, 113, 115, 118, 134, 145, 148, 150, 161
Parry Sound Lumber Company, 92
Parry Sound North Star, 87
Partridge:
    A.W. (Dr.), 121, 124, 126, 127, 129, 130, 132
    Franklin Henry "Skipper," 124–127, 129, 130
    Jean (Partridge), 127, 130
    Julia Ann, 128, 129
    H.L. (Rev.)
Paxton Township (Parry Sound District), 63, 64, 68, 79
Pearce, Bill, 125
Penetang, Penetanguishe (ON), 92
Perry, Township of (Parry Sound District), 54, 55, 117, 151, 161
Perry Township Agricultural Society, 54
Peterborough (ON), 33
Peterson, David, 117

Pettawawa (ON), 68
Peuchen:
    Arthur Godfrey, 74–76
    Eliza Eleanor (Clark) (Mrs. Godfrey), 74
    Godfrey, 74
    Margaret (Thompson) (Mrs. A.G.), 74, 76
Pevensey (ON), 131
Pevensey United Church, 143
Phillips, Billy, 123
Pickerel Landing Village (ON), 92
Pickerel River, 11, 13, 14, 18–20, 77–81, 83–87, 90, 96–102, 104-111
Pickerel River Indian Reserve, 95
Pigeon Lake, 8
Pine Lake Lumber, 92
Playfair, James, 16, 17, 19, 100
Plymouth Brethren Church, 49
Port Carmen, 122
Port Loring (ON), 12, 14, 16, 55, 56, 83, 85, 86, 95, 99, 101, 102, 104, 106, 109–112
Port-of-Loring, see Port Loring
Port Sydney (ON), 34
Powassan (ON), 12, 13, 32, 36, 61, 146, 150
Powell, Baden (Lord), 125, 133
Pritchard, Mike, 107
Provencal, W.G., 72
Prunty, Frank, 137
Pusey, Charles J., 89

Quathiaski Cove (BC), 39
Queen's Own Rifles, 74, 75

Radford, George, 124, 131
Ratz, Ephreum, 102
Ratz, Jacob, 16, 102, 103
Ray Industries Incorporated (Michigan), 73
Red Cross Outpost Hospital (Loring), 55, 56

Red Cross Society, 55, 56, 143
Red Hotel, see Fairview Hotel
Reeds, Arthur, 69
Reeds, Cliff, 134
Reid and Company (Toronto), 89
Restoule (ON), 55
Restoule River, 87
Reynolds, C.W. (Rev.), 140
Rhodes, Chas., 137
Rice Lake, 33
Richmond Hill (ON), 37
Riddell's Tailor Shop (Sundridge), 140
Rillett, __ (Miss). 55
Ristic, Helen, 56, 57
Robert M. Carter Shoe Store (South River), 63
Robertson, Betsy (Dobbs), 82
Robertson, Bob, 65
Robertson, John, 81
Robertson, Robert, 82
Rogerson, Archie, 103
Rogerson's Mill, 103
Roncadin, Rino, 138
Roncadin, Susan (McConkey), 136–138
Roosevelt, Franklin Delano (President), 125
Rosie, Barbara, see Barbara Smith
Ross, John Hugo, 74, 75, 168
Ross, Mary Ann (McConkey), 136–138
Rosseau (ON), 34, 60, 79
Rosseau Falls (ON), 44, 45
Rosseau-Nipissing Colonization Road, 26, 34, 60, 79
Round Lake, 66
Rowell, E.N., 105, 106
Russell, Jack, 45, 154
Rutherford, Dane, 92
Rutherford, Gertie (Laughlin), 93
Ryerson, Township of (Parry Sound District), 157

Sand Lake, 134
Sarares, Jack, 48
Sawyer, Ernest "Ernie," 14, 103, 106, 108
Sawyer, Nellie, 14, 103
Schroeder, John, 17, 19, 100
Schroeder Mills and Timber Company, 13, 17, 85, 92, 95–101, 106–09
Scotia Junction (ON), 54, 55, 5
Scouts Canada, 121, 132
Second World War (WWII), 68, 73, 124, 127, 131
Shannon, __ (Mr.), 62, 63
Sharpe, James, 25, 27
Mr. Sidewand, __ (Mr.), 141
Simcoe (ON), 20
Simpson, Pat, 109
Simpson, Ron, 109
Simp's Landing (Lakeview Hotel), 109
Sims, Charles, 106
Sinclair, A.W., 82
Sir Richard Thomas, 11
Sloan, __ (Dr.), 53
Smith:
    Barbara (Rosie) (Mrs. Donald), 83
    Donald, 83
    Edward J. (Capt.), 74, 75
    John, 56
Smith, Ray (District Commissioner), 121
Smith, Sidney, 143
Smokey Creek Dam, 105
Smyth, William, 63
South River (ON), 55, 63–68, 71–73, 76, 151
South River Lumber Company, 63, 64
South River-Machar Union Public Library, 73
South River Mercantile Company, 63, 64
Sovereign Bank, 64
Spanish Flu, 85, 95, 96, 108
Spears, Carmen, 95

Spears, Joseph, 89, 90, 96
Sprucedale (ON), 51, 124, 125, 131
Squaw Lake, 19, 78
Stamp, Muriel, 95
St. Andrew's Presbyterian Church (Burk's Falls), 122
St. Mary's (ON), 22
St. Thomas (ON), 11, 12, 85
Standard Chemical Company, 61, 64, 69, 71–74, 76
Stanley Byers (tugboat), 106–08, 111
Stanley Lake, 99
Steirerhut Restaurant, 36
Stewart, Harvey, 122
Stevenson, Clarke, 151
Still River, 78, 97
Stirling Falls (ON), 34, 36
Stony Lake/Lake Bernard, 34–36, 143
Strickland, George, 15
Stringer, Dan (Park Ranger), 68, 70, 71
Strong Township of, (Parry Sound District), 36, 131
Stuart and Donnelly Lumber Co., 106
Stumpy Bay, 105
Sturdy, Jane, 82
Sturdy, John, 82
Sturgeon River, 61
Sudbury (ON), 49, 95
Sundridge (ON), 32, 33, 35–39, 41, 45, 55, 108, 139–41, 143, 144, 148, 151, 155
Sundridge Beavers, 145, 146
Sundridge Hardware, 140
Sundridge Lions Club, 145
Sutherland Jean, 150
Sweet, Frank, 105
Sword:
    Annie, 99
    John, 97
    Percy D., 97
    Thomas, 97

Swords (ON), 97

Taylor, Edward Plunket "E.P.," 73
Tedders, __ (Miss), 56
Temagami (ON), 46
Ten Gables Golf Inn (Sundridge), 33, 38
The Alsace (hamlet), 55
Theberge, Greg, 146
The "Elbow" (Pickerel River), 87, 89, 105
The Narrows (Eagle Lake), 62
Theresa (tug boat), 19, 44, 45
Thomas:
    Gladys Gertrude (Brook), 113
    Herbert Edgar, 113
    Jane Anne "Jenny" (Mrs. R.M.), 113, 115, 119, 120
    Nell, 119
    Pandora, 119
    Richard Malcolm, 113, 115–20, 161, 163
    Sarah, 119
Thompson, Art, 122, 124
Thompson, John, 74
Thompson, Margaret, see Margaret Peuchen
Thompson, Ray, 110
Thorpe, Richard J., 16, 29
Timmins (ON), 49, 50
Titanic (ocean liner), 74, 75
Toad Lake, 98, 105
Tobodio, Duncan, 141
Tom Thomson Park (South River), 73
Toronto (ON), 16, 32, 38, 43, 48, 53, 65, 71, 74, 76, 79, 82, 84, 89, 96, 107, 113, 115, 120, 127, 132, 150
Toronto Children's Aid Society, 54
Toronto Humane Society, 53
Toronto Maple Leafs, 146
Trigg, James, 131
Trimmer, H.W., 29
Trimmer's Hotel (Burk's Falls), 29
Trout Creek (ON), 57, 62, 67, 71, 110

Trussler, Hartley, 71
Trussler Bros. Mill, 62
Tulley, __ (Capt.), 109
Turner Bros. Lumber Company (North Bay), 20, 63, 64, 79

Ullman, Norm, 67
United Empire Loyalists, 30
United Nations Institute of Training and Research, 117
Unmarried Parents Act (UP), 53
Upper Canada, 30

Varcoe, Ken, 127
Vancouver (BC), 115
Vancouver Island, 39
Vanello, Ari, 67
VanEvery, John, 83
VanEvery, Owen Herbert, 83
Verda (yacht), 74
Victoria Harbour ()N), 97, 100
Victoria Harbour Lumber Co. 79, 89, 169
Villemaire, Doris (Brazier), 50, 51
Villemaire, Jim, 51
Vincent Company Store (South River), 63
Vrooman, Bill, 151
W.A. Connelly Planing Mill (South River), 63
W.H. Cole and Sons, 89, 105
Wait, Jard (carriage sales/repairs), 63
Walkerton Lumber Co., 77
Walton:
    Arthur (Capt.), 2, 13, 14, 102–06, 111
    Aubrey "Dob" Taylor, 12–14, 87, 103–11
    Bertha, 14, 102
    Carolyn "Carrie" Alberta (Taylor) (Mrs. William), 14, 103, 104, 10
    Daisy Eloise, 14, 103, 109
    Edgar, 2, 13, 102, 106, 105, 109
    Edgar, 14
    Ellen (Patterson), (Mrs. Edgar), 102
    Enid, 102
    Ethel, 14, 102
    Leith Glenister "Bun," 14, 103, 108
    Marjorie "Margery," 14, 102
    Merrill Linwood "Squirrel," 14, 103, 107, 108
    Mildred (Mrs. Dob), 13
    Nellie (Mrs. Edgar), 14
    Rebekah Celesia (Sawyer) (Mrs. Athur), 14, 102
    William, 14
    William (Captain), 2, 13, 14, 102, 104, 108, 110, 111
Wanapitei River, 77
Wanita (steamer), 26, 31, 44
Ward, Elma, see Elma Kirton
Ward, John, 41, 48
Ward, Mary, 41, 48
Ware, Bill, 121
Warner, Ernie "Boss," 121, 122, 126
Wasi Falls (ON), 62
Wasi River, 62
Waterloo (ON), 84
Watte, Gordon, 72
Wauquimakog (Wilson) Lake, 14
Webber, Jim, 123
Welcome Centre (Burk's Falls), 147
Well, Fred, 106
Weller, Wilma, 55
Welsh, Henry, 158
Wenonah (steamer), 25
Wesley, Frank (Mr.), 53
Wesley, Ruth (Mrs. Frank), 53, 128
West & Peachey (Simcoe), 20
West End Supply Depot (South River), 63
Whitby's Tailor Shop (Sundridge), 140
White, Charles, 55
White Eagle Home (Loring), 56

Whitestone Lake, 82
Wilberforce (ON), 89
Wickett, Barney, 65
Wild Cat Rapids, 48
Wiley, Mary (Kirton), 83
Wiley, Wesley, 83
Wilson, Annie, see Annie King
Wilson, Bud, 138
Wilson, Dixie, 111
Wilson. J.J. (Dr.), 58
Wilson, Jack, 123, 124, 131
Wilson, James "Jim," 27, 53, 57
Wilson, John, 27, 59, 131
Wilson, Louise (Mrs. John), 59
Wilson, William, 27, 59
Wilson, Township of (Parry Sound District), 78–80, 93, 92
Wilson Dam, 87, 105
Wilson Lake, 83, 99, 102–05, 109
Wiltshire, __ (Miss), 55
Wisser, Charles, 141
Wittick, Dave, 123
Wittick, Dr. Milton A. (Dr.), 17, 53, 57, 58, 123, 124, 126, 128, 131
Wolf River, 98
Wood, Art, 67
Woodruff, Albert J., 137
Woodstock (ON), 73

Young, Clayton, 127

Zentler, Mona (Miss), 56
Ziehm, Karl, 81

About the Author

Born and raised in Toronto, Astrid thoroughly enjoyed the annual escape from the city to the family's summer cottage in East Parry Sound while she was growing up. The cottage was located on Compass Lake near the hamlet of Sprucedale and those memorable summers spent with her parents were to leave a lasting impression. She quickly learned to appreciate the beauty of the Almaguin Highlands, as the countryside reminded her parents, both refugees from the Second World War, of their homeland, Estonia. Happily, a rustic cabin still sits on the expansive property and today, living so close as she does in the nearby Village of Burk's Falls, trips to the lake with her dog are made on a regular basis.

Astrid's interest in everything to do with history blossomed while attending Victoria University at the University of Toronto. Although she eventually earned her bachelor's degree in fine art, Astrid's involvement with the grassroots conservation group, the Local Architectural Conservation Advisory Committee (LACAC) for the Town of Markham was to take her down a very different path. Before long she became the committee's historical researcher as well as a regular columnist with the weekly *Markham Economist and Sun,* writing about the life and times of the early settlers of Thornhill, Unionville and Markham Villages.

Astrid joined the editorial staff of the Burk's Falls home office of *Almaguin News* (Almaguin Publishing (1989) Limited), and eighteen years later she continues to make her home in this picturesque riverside community. As well as continuing her writing, Astrid lends her support to environmental and humane causes. Her first book was *Almaguin: A Highland History*, published by Natural Heritage books in 1998.

www.ingramcontent.com/pod-product-compliance
Lightning Source LLC
Chambersburg PA
CBHW080412170426
43194CB00015B/2792